CHASING A DREAM

MEMOIRS OF A GOLF PROFESSIONAL

By
Gaines Beard

Other books by Gaines Beard-

The Adventures of Captain Snappy and Little Buddy

Copyright © 2024 by Gaines Beard

ISBN: 9798872845836

Independently published
Cover photo: Gaines Beard
Cover design by Anjli Mehta
All rights reserved. No part of this book may be reproduced in any manner without the express written consent of the author, except in the case of brief excerpts in critical reviews or articles.
Printed in the United States of America
Third Edition: 2024

What Folks Are Saying About

Chasing A Dream: Memoirs of A Golf Professional

Chasing a Dream takes us back to the sixties and seventies when young Gaines catches the golfing bug and thinks he just might be good enough to go pro. Golfers of any level will enjoy this engaging memoir, written in a gentle, folksy style and full of memorable vignettes featuring golfing personalities. Even non-golfers will appreciate and relate to the struggles of a young man trying to make his way in the world, and the intimate peek into the genteel world of Southern living from a bygone era. A great read! EJS

Have you ever had a dream to become the BEST of the BEST in a field of business or sports? If so, you know the journey will be long and hard; many dues to pay; sacrifices to make. In this memoir, Gaines Beard shares his journey to become a golf professional; the commitment needed, financial sacrifices to make, disappointments, hurrahs and people he met along the way who supported and encouraged him to keep going when the going got rough. Within the confines of the professional golfing world where competition is stiff, Gaines maintained his integrity, kindness and most of all the respect of his fellow golfers. Gaines Beard is a rare competitor in the golfing world. Gaines's journey could be YOUR journey. Anyone committed to chasing a dream will be inspired by Gaine's story.
SKW

"Gaines Beard and I met at Possum Trot Golf Club (no joke) in Myrtle Beach, South Carolina, where, as young assistant golf pros, we had the same dream of qualifying for the PGA Tour. In this memoir, with great honesty, Gaines shares his innermost feelings, telling you how he felt he was good enough to play professional golf, and gives readers a glimpse into the hearts and souls of young players all over the world who are chasing that same dream. This memoir gives you a taste of both sides of the dream. I hope you enjoy this book as much as I did. I am today and will always be a good friend to Gaines 'Broke' Beard."

-Leonard Thompson
Leonard had more than 70 top-10 finishes in PGA Tour events during his career. He has played in more than 1100 combined tour events with eight professional wins and career earnings of nearly eight million dollars.

***

Whether you are a golfer or not, you'll find Gaines Beard's Chasing A Dream: Memoirs of a Golf Professional to be a FUN read, period. Gaines spins a colorful tale of his younger years in and around golf and gives us glimpses into the lives of many of the fascinating people he met along the way.

-Dennis McCormac, President of the Golfweek & Senior Amateur Tour

Dedication

I dedicate this book to my brother Bryce, who taught me to play and shared with me his passion for the game. Without him, the events in this book would never have happened.

Bryce   Me

Additional Dedication

I would be remiss if I didn't acknowledge the person who initially introduced Bryce and me to our first set of golf clubs, our grandmother Katherine "Kitty" Murphy.

Circa 1938   Country Club of Salisbury

Preface

I joined a writer's workshop in 2022, wanting to write stories about my life that I could hand down to my grandchildren. Our workshop had several accomplished authors. What started out as one chapter presented to the group for critiquing turned into a burning desire to put my golfing experiences into my memoirs.

My story is unique to me but portions of it are not unfamiliar to the thousands of men and women who have dreamed of playing professional golf.

Contents

Chapter 1: Columbus, Ohio 1

Chapter 2: Brookdale Golf Club 7

Chapter 3: The Shag Boy 21

Chapter 4: Possum Trot Golf Club 37

Chapter 5: Mrs. Baldwin's Cottage 47

Chapter 6: Dreadful News 55

Chapter 7: Starting A Family 67

Chapter 8: Q-School 77

Chapter 9: A Strange Day 83

Chapter 10: Going To the Big Dance 90

Chapter 11: But The Band Didn't Play 100

Chapter 12: Moving On 110

Chapter 13: The Playoff 119

Chapter 14: The Next Chapter 133

Chapter 15: The Dogfight 136

Chapter 16: The Caddy 143

Chapter 17: A Pro's Golf Tips 155

Chapter 1

Columbus, Ohio

When I was eight years old and my brother Bryce eleven, we moved to Ohio with our mother and new stepfather, Seth Murdoch. Seth was a major in the United States Air Force. He had been transferred from Shreveport, Louisiana, to the Strategic Air Command (SAC) division at Lockbourne Air Force Base in Columbus. It was December 20, 1957.

As we drove into our neighborhood, lined with newly constructed houses, snow was falling so thick we could barely see the road ahead of us. There was at least a foot of snow on the ground when we arrived at 14982 Country Club Drive. At that moment, I knew that living in Ohio was going to be fun. I could already see Bryce and me building snow forts and igloos in the front yard and throwing snowballs at the cars and trucks passing by. That first night in our new home, I dreamt of our first white Christmas and hoped Santa would bring me a Red Flexible Flyer sled.

That Christmas, our grandmother Kitty gave us our first set of golf clubs. It was a complete set of Spalding Shelley Mayfield's, consisting of nine irons, a 2-iron through the wedge, and a 1, 2, 3, and 4 wood. There were also two canvas carry bags and two putters.

"Seth," I asked, "why are there two golf bags and two putters but only one set of golf clubs?"

He smiled and answered, "Your grandmother wanted to make sure that you boys liked the game and wanted to play it before she bought y'all a second set." He suggested that we split the clubs up, with one of us taking the even numbered and the other the odd.

Bryce, being the oldest and better in math than I was, said "I'll take the evens," looking at Seth with a smile. It was settled. When we divided up the clubs and put them into our new khaki-colored carry bags, I noticed that Bryce had one more club than I did.

"Hey, how come you get one more club than I do?" Bryce explained, "That is simply how math works, and after all, I am the oldest." He put his hand on my shoulder and said, "Look at it this way; your bag won't be as heavy as mine." That made sense to me, and all was good.

With a foot of snow on the ground, it didn't take long before our clubs made their way into the darkest corner of our closet. They never saw the light of day, and we never played golf in Columbus, but we certainly went to the golf course a bunch of times.

We got a small weekly allowance of fifty cents each. It was decent money, being that a soda was six cents and a candy bar three. However, I had an insatiable passion for candy, especially Sugar Daddy's. Half a dollar just wasn't going to get it, and I was not going to eat into my school milk money to satisfy my sweet tooth. Being an industrious lad, Bryce figured out a couple of ways for us to make some extra money and have fun doing it at the same time. One way was to collect pop bottles from the sides of the road and turn them into the local drug store for the two-cent deposits. Another way was to hunt for golf balls at the south end of Country Club Drive. At the north end, fourteen blocks up, was the Columbus Country Club. On weekends, we would ride my brother's English 3-speed bike those fourteen blocks to the club, me sitting sidesaddle on the middle bar. It wasn't very comfortable, but Bryce bribed me to go along with him by promising to buy me a Fudgesicle at Fox's Drugstore, where we cashed in the pop bottles that we had picked up that day.

The first time we rode to the Country Club was quite an adventure. Bryce peddled the bike along the street and on the sidewalks when the traffic was heavy, stopping at every red light. We lost our balance while waiting for the light to turn green, early into our trip. The bike tipped over, and both of us ended up in the gutter with scraped palms. After that, at each red light, I would dismount the center bar so we wouldn't repeat that embarrassing tumble.

When we finally reached the property boundary of the club, we were not at the club entrance but near one of the fairways several holes away from the clubhouse. There was a six-foot-tall wire fence protecting the club property from intruders. Beyond the fence were woods that bordered one of the fairways. A sign on the fence clearly stated, "Members Only. No Trespassing."

I said, "Bryce, we can't go in there."

"Look, don't worry about that. What are they going to do, throw us in jail? Come on, let's see if we can find a hole in the fence." A few yards down the line, we found an opening in the fence where two sections connected. Bryce said, "OK, now just act like we belong here like any member's kids, and no one will know the difference. Come on, let's go find some golf balls."

It didn't take long before we found about a dozen balls: Spalding Dots, Maxflis, Pinnacles, Club Specials and Po Do's…. I found it interesting that all the balls had numbers on them for identification purposes except the Pinnacles. Instead of a number, they had two painted dots on them next to the Pinnacle imprint. These two dots were of assorted colors and different combinations for their identification. Back then, Golf balls were called balatas because of their construction. In the center of the ball was a small rubber orb, about the size of a marble, filled with liquid. It was tightly wound with a rubber band string with a similar-looking pattern to a wound ball of yarn. It was then covered with a dimpled, soft rubber outer layer. The finished ball was perfectly round and had a lot of bounce. If it were a miss-hit, say with the sharp leading edge of the golf club, it was easy to crease open, exposing the rubber band inside, making it unplayable.

Golfers would often have to replace their ball during a round. New golf balls cost $1.75 for a sleeve of three in the pro shop. We could sell used balls for .10 to .25 cents each, depending on the condition of the covers. Finding and selling used balls became a very profitable enterprise. We would sit along the edge of the woods, where we could be seen by the golfers passing by. We had the balls laid out on the ground in front of us for them to look through. It didn't take long to sell all the balls that we found.

On that first day, we headed back down those fourteen blocks with $2.35 in our pocket. With the ten or so pop bottles we found, we had made, in one afternoon, more money than we could have made by mowing lawns or babysitting. From that day on, ball hunting became our regular Saturday activity.

One evening at supper, our stepfather Seth said to Bryce, "You know, Bryce, if you are interested in learning how to play golf, one of the best ways to learn is to start off by caddying. Caddying is a great way to see, up close, how the game is played."

Bryce said, "But I don't know anything about caddying." Seth went on to explain that it was simple. He said that the caddy carries the golf bag for the player while staying out of his or her way and not talking unless spoken to. Sometimes, he would have to rake the sand smoothly in the sand traps after the player hit a shot out of it.

Bryce took Seth's advice and rode his bike to the club on weekends to hang out around the caddy area near the pro shop with hopes that someone would need his caddy services. Club member's children were not allowed to be caddies. The golf pro welcomed Bryce and other non-member young men to be caddies at the club. He even gave them basic instructions on what was expected of them, where they could and could not go while on club property, dress codes, etc. Motorized golf carts had yet to be widely introduced to the game of golf; therefore, caddying was a needed service at many golf courses.

Bryce caddied that summer, making two-to-three dollars a day. He would come home with stories about the interesting people he had met. One Saturday, Bryce came home all excited and he had caddied for a nineteen-year-old college golfer who played on the Ohio State University golf team. He was the best golfer Bryce had ever seen. He said the young man hit booming drives that went nearly 300 yards, and his iron shots had the accuracy of a dart thrower.

After the round, the young man asked Bryce if he would shag balls for him so he could get in some extra practice. Shagging balls was simply going out on the practice area and letting the player hit balls to you. You would then collect the balls in a "shag bag" and return them to the player. It was a fun exercise and interesting to see the ball flying in the air toward you. The shag bag was very similar to a bowling ball bag, and it was fun to try to catch the ball in the bag before it hit the ground.

Bryce caddied a few more times for the young man that summer. His demeanor and confidence, along with his incredible talent, convinced my brother that he would be famous someday. Bryce said his name was Jack Nicklaus.

Chapter 2

Brookdale Golf Club

I can remember it like it was yesterday…the night that changed our lives forever!

It was one of those warm summer nights that seemed made for front porch sitting. It was Saturday, May 25th, 1968, two weeks before my graduation from Boyden High School in my hometown of Salisbury, NC. My grandparents' home was on W. Bank Street in the heart of the historic district. It was a beautiful example of a Greek Revival style with two verandas, as my mother called them, one upstairs and one downstairs. They stretched the width of the house and had six large white columns across the front.

229 West Bank Street

Chasing A Dream

I had just returned home from a Friday night date to the movies with my best girl, Linda Ketner. Linda's father and uncle had a few grocery stores with plans to expand. Little did anyone dream that their small Food Town Grocers would, in coming years, become one of the largest food chains in the country.

I grabbed a beer and sat on the glider sofa on the front porch, waiting for my older brother, Bryce to return home after a night out with the boys. Bryce was a junior at the University of North Carolina at Chapel Hill.

As was usual in our neighborhood, after 10 o'clock in the evening, few cars drove by our home. The old town was asleep in the quiet of the night. I could hear crickets and the occasional chant of katydids through the large crepe myrtles that had adorned our front lawn for nearly a century. In the distance, the sound of the Southern Crescent Train could be heard as it passed through town on its daily trip from NY and Washington D.C. to Atlanta and New Orleans. Its whistle blew as it approached the crossings in our beautiful, historic town.

It was a crisp night in late May. The flowers and trees were in bloom, and the sweet fragrance of the majestic magnolias and gardenias permeated my senses and reminded me of my grandmother Kitty's cologne. For the first time this spring, lightning bugs darted their way around the yard. It was a glorious night with the moon fully aglow.

Around 11:00 p.m., Bryce returned home, and with him was our mutual best friend, Brian Nussman. It didn't take long for me to realize that Bryce and Brian had been out drinking with the boys because Brian still had a half-full bottle of Ancient Age bourbon in his hand. We sat on the porch and talked about our evening while passing the bottle around. At eighteen, I had yet to develop a taste for hard liquor. It wasn't long until the bottle was empty, and my balance challenged.

Brian and Bryce were both twenty-one and had been pals for years. When they graduated high school three years earlier, Bryce went off to Chapel Hill while Brian headed to Boone, NC, to attend Appalachian State Teacher's College. As Bryce tells it, Brian had no desire to become a teacher and had no desire to attend college at all. He was forced to go by his parents even though everyone knew that he would end up some day working for his family-owned lumber company. Bryce said that the only reason Brian chose Appalachian State was because the girl-to-boy ratio there was eight to one.

It didn't take long before Brian hit the grand slam. He succeeded in recording four "D's" and an incomplete in PE in his second semester. Brian was summoned home to work in the sawmill. Once home, he realized that all his buddies were off at college, so he gravitated toward me for fun and games until his friends came home for summer vacation.

We developed a close friendship. Brian mentored me in the ways of girls and helped me to refine my skills of endurance regarding Miller High Life, The Champagne of Bottled Beers.

Bryan and my mutual friends were all country clubbers. Our families had been members of the Country Club of Salisbury since 1920 when my grandfather, Bryce Parker Beard, Sr., and several other prominent businessmen, beckoned the-then renouned Scottish golf course architect, Donald Ross, to come to Salisbury to design our course. Over the years, the Country Club of Salisbury has become recognized as one of the finest clubs in the state, not just for its challenging golf course but also for its elegant facilities and southern charm.

Chasing A Dream

    I don't recall whose brilliant idea it was to drive out to Brookdale Golf Club at midnight to play moon golf on their nine-hole, par three golf course, but it sounded like a good idea at the time. Bryce, Brian, and I piled into my brother's 1966 Pontiac Bonneville convertible and headed to Brookdale, about a mile outside of the city limits. As we crossed over the railroad tracks and under the new I-85 overpass at the edge of town, there wasn't a single car in sight. It was a beautiful moonlit summer night when we arrived at Brookdale. Bryce opened the trunk, and to our surprise, he had not put his clubs back in the car after golfing at the club earlier that day.

    Drunk and seeing no other alternative, we devised a plan to break into the golf shop and borrow a couple clubs to use that night. It seemed a logical plan knowing that the owner of Brookdale, Gaither McCombs, was an old family friend and an occasional bridge partner of our grandmother, Kitty Murphy.

    With me being the smallest of the three, Bryce and Brian hoisted me up to a window at the rear of the club. I broke a small windowpane under the latch, opened the window, and shimmied in. I found a light switch and opened the front door.

    We left Gaither a note explaining that we had been drinking and couldn't resist the challenge of playing in the World Championship of Moon Golf. We said that we would come back in the morning and replace the broken glass, pay for the balls, and Miller High Life. We would leave the borrowed clubs there when we finished playing.

    When we got into the car to drive over to the first tee, we saw blue lights suddenly speeding in on us from both directions on the dirt road. It looked like a scene from Smokey and the Bandit with all the dust and gravel flying everywhere in the headlights. Brian begged me and Bryce to say that he was not involved with the break-in and say he passed out in the back seat of the car. Brian's father was a strict disciplinarian, and Brian had seen his anger before. I'm not sure who was the most scared, however. Our stepfather, Seth, was the Rowan County Manager and was tightly involved with the sheriff's department, whose offices were also located in the same courthouse building.

To make matters even worse, our grandfather, Spencer, was editor of The Salisbury Evening Post for thirty-four years, and our grandmother, Kitty, was the advertising manager for the local radio station. In retrospect, I think I would rather have had Brian's dad's anger over the embarrassment and shame we were about to cause our family.

Four patrol cars swooped down on us. You would have thought that we had broken into Ft. Knox. What happened next is almost too hard to believe. Two of the deputies approached our car, and the other two, with flashlights, went to inspect the outside of the golf shop.

Bryce rolled down his window and said, "Good evening, officer." The deputy replied that it was 1:30 in the morning and asked us to get out of the car. Bryce and I opened our doors and got out while Brian sat motionless, leaning against his door in the back seat. The second deputy opened Brian's door, and he rolled out of the car and down an embankment into a drainage ditch full of water.

Brian stumbled up and asked, "What's going on? Where the hell am I?"

The other two deputies returned and said they had not seen any signs of a break-in. After obtaining our IDs, we were put into three different patrol cars. The four deputies went to do another inspection. Scared and alone, we sat waiting for the bad news that was sure to come from the second inspection.

The silence was broken when over the patrol car radio came this voice ranting and raving stupid shit like "Who do they think they are?" and "My daddy can buy and sell Sheriff Stirewalt!"

At the top of my lungs, I was screaming for Brian to shut the fuck up, and I found out later, so was Bryce, but Brian could not hear us. It turns out that the deputy of Brian's car had "accidentally" left the mic on.

The four returned with the news that they had found the broken pane. Luckily, they had not heard Brian's rantings. When we arrived at the sheriff's office, we were met by Brookdale's owner, Gaither McCombs, and Homer Lucas, who covered the police beat for The Salisbury Evening Post. The latter two were shaking their heads in disbelief. Gaither explained that he did not want to press charges because he knew us. He said that he knew that we would repair the broken glass in the morning and considered the incident an unfortunate boyhood prank gone awry. They released us into Homer's custody to drive us home.

In the morning, Bryce walked over to Brian's house, and he and Brian's father drove to the lumber company to get tools and a few panes of glass. They drove out to Brookdale and replaced the glass, made their apologies, and again thanked Gaither profusely for his understanding.

Bryce picked up his car, still parked alongside the road, and drove home to the beautiful sounds of the church bells chiming that the 10:00 a.m. services were about to commence. When Bryce got home, he said, "I think we may have dodged a bullet for the time being. I'm sure Seth will find out first thing tomorrow morning."

It was around noon when the phone rang. It was Brian calling to say that the dispatcher at the sheriff's office had called to tell Brian to pick us up and come to the office at 2:00 p.m. that afternoon because Sheriff Stirewalt wanted to talk with us. Brian picked us up, and we slowly drove the three blocks to the courthouse. Bryce said that it was a sure bet that the rantings of Brian the night before had reached the sheriff. We felt like lambs on the way to the slaughterhouse.

We knew it was bad when we entered the sheriff's office and once again saw Gaither McCombs. Sheriff Stirewalt gave us an unnerving stare as we approached the desk. In his hand, he held out an arrest complaint for Gaither to sign in our presence.

We knew that Gaither felt otherwise but realized that the sheriff must have pressured him. The three of us were fingerprinted and released into the custody of our parents to await trial.

When we got outside, Gaither was waiting in his car. He explained that Sheriff Stirewalt told him in no uncertain terms that if he wanted the quick response of his department to any future silent alarms from Brookdale, it would be wise to file charges this time. Gaither said, "Boys, you know I didn't want to do this; Sheriff Stirewalt was not amused and seemed really pissed at you boys."

Homer had called Seth and my mother from the sheriff's office to tell them the news. That afternoon, our mother was sitting in the glider out on the front porch with a Salem cigarette in one hand and bourbon and water in the other.

As we walked up onto the porch, she said, "It will be your pleasure to have a seat!" She commenced into an ass-chewing that would make a prison warden proud. The "What the Hell were y'all thinking?" and "How could you embarrass your family like this, especially with your grandmother lying over there in the hospital, dying of cancer?" and so on. When she successfully had us cowering with shame, she allowed the following to be fact:

"You two fools are going to take your medicine like gentlemen. Don't think for a second that your stepfather nor I are going to waste our hard-earned money paying for an attorney for you. When the day comes, y'all are going to march your asses down to that courthouse and throw yourselves on the mercy of the court and plead "No Lo Contendre" and let the chips fall where they may. I'm not going to allow the two of you to cause more embarrassment for this family." She ended by saying, "Now you both go up to your rooms without supper."

On Monday afternoon, Seth returned home with the information that our court date had been set for Wednesday week at 10:00 a.m., just two days before I was to graduate from high school.

Up until my senior year, before moving back to Salisbury, I had been a very good student and had scored 1250 on my SATs despite staying up the night before the test drinking. We had spent most evenings of my senior year at Al's Night Hawk Drive-in, near Catawba College, drinking beer or cruising Main Street chasing girls.

The news of our arrest made it into the Monday afternoon paper. I must say that the last two weeks of my high school year were very nerve-racking. One of my teachers, Mary Nicholson, or Mama Nick, as we called her, stopped me in a hallway filled with students and asked, "What do you think your grandfather, Spencer, would think of you right now? How do you think he would feel about the way you have squandered away your education this year?"

He and Ms. Nicolson had been dear friends until his death in 1964 of colon cancer. With her finger wagging just inches from my face, I felt about three feet tall. The only thing missing from her dressing me down was the ear-pulling.

On June 5th, the morning of our court date, I was up early, getting dressed in my best suit and tie and shining my Bass Weejun penny loafers. I even replaced the existing penny with a newly minted 1968 Lincoln cent I had on my dresser for luck. Our trial was to start at 10:00 a.m., and my mother insisted I go to school at 8:00 and then leave for the courthouse at 9:30. She called the office at Boyden High to have me paged over the intercom at 9:20 sharp, just as the first period was starting. It was her way of humiliating to me for what we had done to her.

I was sure all eyes would be on me at school that morning. But upon arrival, everyone was looking strangely sad. Girls were crying, and boyfriends were consoling. Bobby Kennedy had been shot 12 hours earlier in the kitchen of the Ambassador Hotel. For the hour and 20 minutes that I was in school that morning, no one was concerned about me. At 9:45, we met in the hallway outside the courtroom; Bryce, Brian, me, and Brian's lawyer.

Brian had continued his fairy tale about being passed out in the back seat, innocent of the actual B&E. His dad bought his story and hired an attorney to press for Conspiracy to Commit vs. the B&E. His attorney was in the hallway chatting with a deputy friend of his. He later walked over to Brian and said, "Brian, it is my opinion you plead guilty like

Bryce and Gaines because I hear that the prosecution has audio recordings..." (Brian's heart leaped) "...of the three of you inside the Pro Shop. I will still be there to provide moral support and help translate and legalese for you, agreed?" Brian slowly nodded his head and realized he would have to face the music when he got home.

The prosecuting attorney in our trial was none other than Robert Sommers, Jr. Esq., the district attorney himself. It seemed strange that he would oversee this case instead of passing it along to an assistant DA. The three of us and Bob were friends and occasional golf partners. Bob lived beside the second tee box at the Country Club of Salisbury.

The judge that morning was the Honorable Odell Sapp, who incidentally was a dear friend of our grandparents and was a frequent bridge partner of Kitty's.

The courtroom was sparse that morning. Homer, the reporter for the paper, was seated in the back row near the hallway. We took our seats at the defense table and noted that the small population in the courtroom was preoccupied with whispering and expressing sadness at the news of Bobby's assassination.

The trial started with "all rise." We stood and heard the charges against us and were asked how we plead.

Brian, with his attorney by his side, replied, "Guilty, Your Honor."

Bryce replied, "Guilty, Your Honor."
I replied, "No-Lo Contendre, Your Honor." I saw a slight grin on Judge Sapp's face as he turned to Bob Sommers and instructed him to present the evidence against us. That was the only time Judge Sapp smiled that morning.

Bob relayed the facts of the evening in question - the early night drinking, porch sitting, no clubs in the truck, etc. - as if he were one of our lawyers. He gave an account of what had transpired that evening. Incredibly, when Bob finished presenting the evidence, he said in conclusion, "Your Honor, these three boys come from good families and have thrown themselves on the mercy of this court. They are good boys and have never been in trouble with the law before. They had been drinking, and this was not a premeditated crime. I ask the court to be lenient. The prosecution rests."

At that moment, I realized why Bob Sommers had taken the case to prosecute. There was no reason for the prosecution to produce any witnesses that morning. We were pleading guilty, and the case was airtight. The judge turned to Brian's lawyer and asked if the defense had anything it wanted to say before the court handed down its sentencing. He stood up, clearing his throat as he straightened his tie. Almost verbatim, he repeated the earlier plea for leniency given to the court by the district attorney.

The judge thanked him and asked us to rise. My heart was racing, and I was scared shitless for the first time in my life. I didn't know if Judge Sapp would be harsh because it was an election year or lenient because of family ties. Judge Sapp sat staring down at us with his chin in his hand for what seemed an eternity before straightening up and saying, "You boys should be ashamed of yourselves! This may seem little more than a prank to y'all, but I assure you that breaking and entering is no laughing matter to the law. Do you realize that if someone had been living upstairs above the golf shop (as was the case at McCanless Golf Club, a mile down the road from Brookdale) that you would not be standing before me in Municipal Court today? You would, instead, be awaiting trial in Federal Court charged with felony breaking and entering, which carries a minimum three to five years sentence in a state prison. The embarrassment you boys have caused your families should be punishment enough, but this is a court of law, and we have rules we must follow," he paused a moment and took a sip of water.

"As for your being intoxicated, I have heard no evidence to indicate that someone else poured that liquor down your throat. Therefore, it is the decision of this court that the three defendants, being found guilty, be sentenced to two years' incarceration, to be served at Piedmont Correctional Facility." My heart stopped. I could not believe my ears!! *WHAT? PRISON?* Then I heard the greatest word in the English language: "Suspended."

The rest is a blur, but the result was that we had to pay court costs, do forty hours of community service, and report Monday morning to Mr. Hollis Hinkle, our parole officer, for the next two years. Bobby Kennedy died that afternoon. I graduated from high school that Friday.

Monday morning at 9:00, Bryce and I went back to the courthouse, but this time to a small office in the basement. That is where we met, for the first time, Mr. Hollis Hinkle, our parole officer. His office was also in the courthouse, as the county manager's office, our stepfather. We exchanged pleasantries, sat down, and began answering questions that Hollis was reading from a form. The questions went like: "Are your parents living together? How many children are in the home? How many rooms are there in your house?"

After forty-five minutes with Hollis discussing things he already knew, we were released and told to come back in one month.

It was either Wednesday or Thursday evening that week when Bryce and I came home around 7:00 p.m. after playing golf at the club. Seth and Mary Marshall, as Seth referred to my mother, were sitting in the library listening to records and having their usual evening cocktails; Mom a tall glass of Ten High bourbon and water and Seth a Beefeater's gin and tonic.

Seth asked us to come in and take a seat- he had something he wanted to tell us. Apparently, earlier in the week, Hollis Hinkle had a discussion with Judge Sapp. The result was that both agreed that we were not threats to society and that any future Monday morning meetings would just be a waste of Hollis' time. Seth went further to say, "Boys, Odell said that if y'all keep your noses clean and keep this information to yourselves, in six months, your records will be expunged."

We were going to be free as birds with clean records as if it had never happened, with one major exception; as soon as that gavel came down in court that day, our draft status changed from 1-A to 4-F.

A 4-F draft status means one can't be drafted into the military unless our shores are being attacked. It also meant that in September, when Bryce returned as a senior at Chapel Hill, he would be dishonorably discharged from the Air Force ROTC.

With Vietnam at its height in 1968-69, Bryce surely would have had to go to war upon graduation. That drunken prank on that warm May evening, I am certain, saved my brother's life and possibly mine as well.

Chasing A Dream

Later that summer, local golf tournaments were very popular and in full swing. Brookdale's Club Championship was scheduled for the last weekend in July. Bryce dared me to play in the Brookdale Club Championship, open to all male golfers in Rowan County. Never being one who could resist a good dare, I entered the tournament, won four straight head-to-head matches, and won the club championship in broad daylight.

WINNER AND RUNNER-UP — Gaines Beard, left, receives the Brookdale Spring golf tourney championship after edging Wade Benfield, right, by 2-up in the finals yesterday. (Staff Photo).

Beard Captures Brookdale Event

Courtesy of The Salisbury Post

Chapter 3

The Shag Boy

I was standing in the pro shop at the Country Club of Salisbury one January afternoon. The club was where most of us junior golfers went after school to play nine holes, practice our putting and chipping, hit range balls, or just hang out with our buddies. It was also the only place in town where we charged food and snacks to our parent's account.

Our pro, Gene Thompson was talking about the excitement that was stirring at the club over the news that, once again, Byron Nelson and Arnold Palmer would return to the Country Club of Salisbury to participate in a golf exhibition for the National Sportscasters and Sportswriters Association's (NSSA) Annual Awards Ceremony.

The NSSA was the brainchild of a local Salisbury restaurant owner, Pete DeMizzio, who began honoring sportswriters he had met in Greensboro at the Greater Greensboro Open in 1953. A few years later, the association was to include radio and television sportscasters. The NSSA grew to over 1,100 due-paying members. Today, it is called The National Sports Media Association.

Every spring, sportswriters, journalists, and radio and television sportscasters from all fifty states would arrive for their moment in the sun. It was an honor to be recognized nationally as the best in their field by their state. Names like Roone Arledge, Producer of ABC's Wide World of Sports, Chris Schinkle, sportscaster, and the like attended the NSSA Annual Awards.

Adding to the excitement of the week was the fact that each year, they invite a famous personality to speak at the awards banquet/ceremony on Sunday night in the Kepple Auditorium at Catawba College. This year's emcee would be Bob Hope, who follows a list of celebrities like John Wayne, Andy Griffith, and Dean Martin. I sensed Gene's excitement about the upcoming event that April and realized how great this was for our local economy and another huge opportunity to showcase Salisbury's southern hospitality to the rest of the country.

I began thinking about the golf exhibition and asked Gene, "How does the exhibition thing work with Byron and Arnie?"

He said, "Byron and Arnold have done this for a couple of years now. Each year, they bring along with them a lady golfer from the LPGA to showcase her talent and help raise awareness and interest in the female golfers. This year, they are bringing Sharron Moran."

"They hit balls on the range, and that's it?" I asked.

"No, the range isn't big enough to accommodate the crowd that will be watching the exhibition. Anyway, our driving range isn't long enough for Arnie's length off the tee." Gene continued, "We set up a hitting area at the ladies' tee on number ten overlooking the tenth fairway in the valley below. There is a loudspeaker set up for Arnie and Byron to use to narrate the shots being hit and to add their own color commentary, which is always entertaining. After the exhibition, which starts at 10:00 a.m., all the dignitaries go into the club ballroom for brunch. After brunch, many of them go out and play in an eighteen-hole Captain's Choice tournament. Arnold, Byron, and Sharron ride around in a cart and hit a few shots with each foursome, sign autographs and get their pictures taken with the group."

I thought how cool it must be to stand there and watch Arnie hit a tee shot for your foursome and get his autograph.

"Gene," I asked, "who goes and picks up all the golf balls in the tenth fairway after the exhibition?"

"No one, Gaines," he replied. "They hit the balls to a shag boy."

I knew what a shag boy was because I had shagged balls for my brother Bryce since I was twelve years old.

I asked, "Who's going to be the shag boy this year?"

Gene looked at me smiling and said, "Gaines, I guess you are…"

"What?" I exclaimed"

"Yes," he said, "if you want to… You are the first to ask…."

You would have thought I had won the lottery. I'm not sure, but I think I even jumped for joy like a little boy on Christmas morning, seeing his first bicycle under the tree.

Gene was the consummate golf professional and had been an assistant pro under none other than Sam Snead in West Virginia earlier in his career. He was also an excellent merchandiser, with new clothing and golf equipment constantly on display in his golf shop. He had just received boxes full of new spring golf apparel and hadn't time to unpack and price the shirts, slacks, and sweaters that would adorn his shelves in the weeks to come.

As a clever merchandiser, Gene naturally stocked a couple lines of Arnold Palmer's brand, recognized the world over by its red, white, green, and yellow umbrella logo proudly embroidered on every garment. I grabbed a medium Arnold Palmer polo shirt from a box in the corner, still in the plastic wrapper, to wear the next day.

I spent much of that spring researching the golf accomplishments of the three stars that would be here in April, just weeks prior to the Masters Tournament in Augusta, GA. I wanted to learn all I could about them so I could fully appreciate the opportunity I'd been given. I didn't have to do much research on Arnie or Byron. Anyone who knew anything about the game of golf knew about "The King" and Arnie's army.

Arnie's army is what the press penned to describe the throngs of fans that adored and followed Arnold Palmer, the most popular golfer to ever live. Arnie was thirty-nine years old and had played thirteen years of professional golf in a fashion unlike anyone before. He had just reached $1,000,000 in career earnings, the first golfer to do so.

Lord Byron, as he was fondly known, was fifty-six years old. Byron had retired from competitive golf at the young age of thirty-four to take up his passion as a gentleman rancher in Texas. In 1945, he won eleven PGA Tournaments in a row and eighteen for the year, a feat that would never again be matched. In 1946, Byron's stroke average was 68.33, which is equal to shooting three under par on every round of the year.

I knew very little about Sharron Moran, the current Rookie of the Year on the LPGA tour. She was a graduate of both the University of Arizona in 1964 and San Diego State in 1965. She had an excellent amateur record, and just before turning pro, Golf Digest voted her the "World's Most Beautiful Golfer." She quickly became known as the beautiful blond with flowing ribboned hats, a five-foot-five-inch, blue-eyed, shapely beauty who could hit a golf ball.

The awards week was a very big deal for the Salisbury Evening Post, where my grandfather, Spencer Murphy, had been editor for thirty-four years. The publisher of our paper was Jimmy Hurley, an avid golfer with an incredible knowledge and love of the game and its inherent quality of ethics and fair play. He admired the game more for its character-building qualities than for its difficulty in mastering. Jimmy would say that you can learn more about a person's character in three hours on the golf course than you can in years of a casual friendship.

The Salisbury Post had a policy of covering every local golf tournament in Rowan County. They would send its sports reporter, Horace Billings, along with a photographer, to report the results of every local tournament. Golf was big in Rowan County.

Mr. Hurley and my family were naturally very close. A week before the Sunday night gala at Catawba College, Mr. Hurley invited me to attend the awards ceremony as his guest.

NSSA week finally arrived!

The night of the ceremony, it was raining cats and dogs. The forecast was for more rain through Monday morning. I asked Mr. Hurley if the exhibition had ever been canceled due to the weather. He assured me that the show would go on unless there was lightning. People would certainly brave the weather for a chance to see the "King" in person.

Monday morning, I awoke bright and early to see the skies dark grey and rain still falling. I got up, showered, shaved, and put on my best pair of golf slacks and, naturally, my brand-new Arnold Palmer golf shirt fresh out of the package. I even spit-shined my best pair of Etonic golf spikes. I was charging full steam ahead with hopes that Mr. Hurley was right about the show going on.

"The show would go on!" The phrase echoed in my head: "show." That was the first time I realized that the exhibition was indeed a show and I, in a small way, would be part of it!

As I was about to head out the front door on my way to the club, I heard my mother laugh from our library, a fabulously comfortable den adjacent to the front hall. "Gaines, come in here for a second." I turned and entered the library, where she often took her morning coffee. As I entered, she took a pair of scissors from the top drawer of an antique desk and asked me to turn around. She skipped off the tag hanging from the back of the collar of my new Arnold Palmer shirt, straightened my collar, kissed me on the cheek and said, "Break a leg."

When I arrived at the club an hour before show time, I noticed that there was a huge Summersett Funeral Home tent that covered the entire ladies' tee on the tenth hole. Unless there was lightning, the show would go on. With Byron, Arnie, and Sharron staying dry under the tent and the patrons under their umbrellas, apparently, the only one guaranteed to get wet that morning would be me. I didn't care in the least. I went into the pro shop to see Gene and get my marching orders for that morning.

Sitting on the counter was a brand spanking new white and burgundy leather shag bag, which resembled a bowling ball bag. It was filled with new Arnold Palmer/Lincoln Mercury golf balls. It had the Arnold Palmer umbrella embroidered on it. Gene picked up the bag, handed it to me and told me to follow him over to the 10th tee. The rain had subsided, and the sky was dark. Gene showed me where the pros would hit from and where to pour out the balls.

"Gene, so what is the procedure?" I asked.

He replied, "At ten, the three of them will be here under the tent. There will be general introductions, thanks, etc., to Lincoln Mercury for bringing these pros to the awards. As is customary, ladies first. Sharron will begin the exhibition by hitting a few wedge shots. You will take the shag bag down the hill and continue about eighty yards. Sharron will aim at you like you are the pin. Pay attention to what you hear from Arnie or Byron on the loudspeaker as she changes clubs and hurry to be ready for the next few shots. After that, you'll get the idea. Please keep your eyes on the ball. These pros are accurate, and they are trying to hit you!"

I understood and prayed, once again, for the rain to hold off. A few minutes before 10:00, the three pros arrived with much fanfare. I was under the tent with Gene as they made their way through the crowd to get ready for the exhibition. Volunteers from Lincoln-Mercury were trailing behind them with their golf clubs. Gene introduced me to them as one of his high school golfers.

There stood Sharron Moran wearing her ribboned chapeau with matching skirt and blouse. She was truly a sight to behold. Byron Nelson was wearing his trademark hat. He was a perfect example of a Southern gentleman.

My heart leaped when I first saw Arnold Palmer. He extended his hand and said, "Hi, I'm Arnold Palmer, what's your name, son?" I told him, and he said, "It's nice to meet you." Then, with a wink, he said, "We are going to have some fun this morning."

Here was my hero talking with me and calling me son! I was on cloud nine. He was more handsome in person with his boyish widow's peak and million-dollar smile. I noticed that Arnie's arms looked like Popeye's, and he had hands like ham hocks, muscular and strong. At 10:00 a.m., you would have known that Arnold Palmer was indeed in town. Hundreds of people were gathered around the 10th tee box. I doubt there was a store in town that didn't have a "Back in an hour" sign hanging in its window. I saw my mother and stepfather in the crowd. Many of the onlookers were as excited to see Sharron as they were to see Arnie and Byron. Some even more so, I was certain.

As Arnie introduced Sharron to the crowd, Gene motioned for me to head off down the hill. The ground was saturated with the two inches of rain we had had the night before. I was glad that I had on golf spikes as I nearly slipped on my ass twice, jogging down the hill. My newly shined Etonics were already a mess. I ran eighty or so yards to the center of the fairway, trying my best to dodge the standing "casual water" puddles along the way.

I was in position with my eyes focused on the top of the hill when I heard Arnie say, "Sharron, how about showing us a few wedge shots?" It was game on, and I was in the game! She struck the first ball high in the sky straight at me. With the gray skies, it was easy to see the ball in the air. It landed about ten feet in front of me, but instead of bouncing, it plugged. I picked up the muddy ball and remarked to myself what a shame it was to put this messy thing in that beautiful new shag bag.

I decided then and there that I would do what I had done for years shagging for my brother. I would catch the balls with the bag. Her next shot was pushed a little to my left. I had time to take three steps and pull open the two leather hoop straps, making the top of the bag look like a giant largemouth bass. The ball landed solidly in the center of the "basket." I heard some clapping, and I swear I thought I saw Sharron tip her hat to me with her left hand. She hit about 20 more shots, some mid to long irons and a couple of drivers.

Soon, I heard Arnie announce Byron Nelson. I had to jog 150 or so yards back to begin shagging for Byron. He hit some wedges that I caught on the fly in the open shag bag. After three shots, he then moved to the seven iron. He was a master at working the ball, fading, or drawing it at will. I will never forget the sound of his irons striking the golf ball. It made a clean, crisp "click" when he hit it. It sounded so pure. As Byron progressed through the bag down to the driver, I noticed that I could see the ball leave the funeral tent before I heard the click. After about fifteen minutes shagging for Mr. Nelson, it was finally Arnie's turn.

Once again, I sloshed my way back to the one-hundred-yard starting place. Out of breath, I saw Arnie's first wedge land past me a good thirty yards. I heard people laughing as I retreated to retrieve the muddy ball. Arnie went through his bag as Byron challenged him to "cut one, draw a couple, how about the punch shot?" and so on. When Arnie finally got to the driver, I turned and ran fifty yards further down the fairway. I was now only a couple of yards short of the tenth green, about 280 yards from the tee. I didn't want him to fly this one over my head. He hit a couple of drives that landed about 15 yards short of me, plugging into the sod. Then I heard Byron say over the loudspeaker, "Arnie, how about one last drive? Draw one in there on him!"

As long as I live, I'll never forget what happened next. I saw Arnie take his trademark mighty swing. The ball rocketed a good fifty yards before I heard the click of the club. It was a solid bullet curving gracefully in from my left and heading directly at me.

There I stood, frozen, like a deer in the headlights, with the shag bag in my right hand. The ball was heading right at me! I was prepared to jump out of the way if it looked like it was going to hit me. As it turned out, I didn't have to move an inch. The ball came in on a low trajectory, and when it hit the ground, it didn't plug in like the rest. Instead, it skipped after plowing a 6" strip through the muck, losing all its speed. It bounced low toward my chest and, in one simple motion, landed squarely in the palm of my left hand. I raised up my hand and waved that ball to the crowd. I could hear them screaming and applauding me and Arnie.

There were joyful tears in my eyes as I headed back towards the tee box. As I walked, I reflected on the magical moment that had just occurred. Imagine catching Arnold Palmer's drive on the first bounce, bare-handed, without moving a muscle. That ball didn't make it to the shag bag. I wanted Arnie to autograph it.

When I got back to the tent, people were everywhere, trying to get autographs from the famous people in attendance.

Mr. Palmer motioned me over and, shaking my hand, said, "Thank you, Gaines, you did a great job!" I then asked him to autograph the ball and my shirt collar.

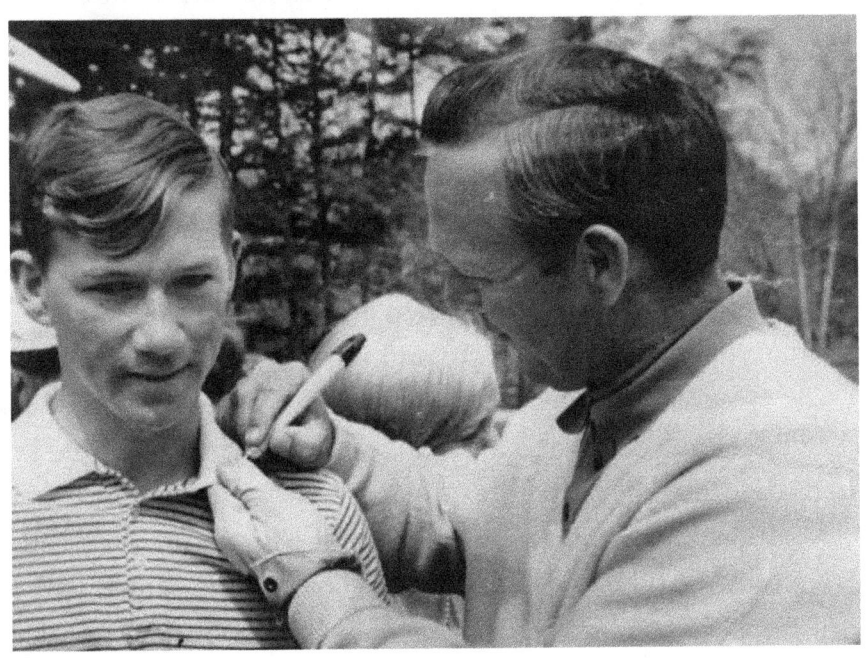

Courtesy The Salisbury Post

Mr. Nelson walked over to me and, with a big smile and handshake, said, "Young man, that may be one of the best displays of shagging I have ever seen."

I was stunned, and all I could come up with was, "Thank you, Mr. Nelson. Where should I put these balls?"

Byron put his hand on my shoulder and said, "Keep them as a token of our appreciation. You helped make this gloomy day brighter. Great job."

"Thank you!" I said. He winked and said I should go up to the clubhouse and grab some brunch. I hesitated and said, "But Mr. Nelson, that's for the NSSA people and other dignitaries."

He said, "Son, come with me."

We walked together to the clubhouse and into the ballroom. He led me to the head of the line. It was like the Red Sea parting as he handed me a plate and said, "Get yourself something to eat." He then turned and had a conversation with a sportswriter. I fixed my plate and noticed that there were place cards arranged on the clothed tables. I certainly could not eat in the ballroom, so I turned and walked to a staircase that led down to the grill and locker rooms.

The grill room was not open on Mondays, and the lights were out. I sat down on the steps about halfway down and with my plate in my lap, closing my eyes while reflecting on that magical morning. After a few minutes of grinning and shaking my head in disbelief, I suddenly felt a tap on my right shoulder.

In a familiar Texas drawl, I heard the words, "Do you mind if I join you?" I looked up, and there he stood with a plate in hand, Lord Byron himself.

Byron thanked me once again. He asked me what my name was and if I was from Salisbury. As we ate, I told him about being an Air Force brat and moving all over the country, including Wichita Falls, Texas. I told him that when I was thirteen and living in Cheyenne, Wyoming, my brother and I got jobs with the pro at the Cheyenne Country Club as shop boys.

"We would pull the members' cart bags from the storage room in the mornings and line them up in order of tee times. In the afternoons, we would wash their clubs and return the carts to the storage racks. We picked up the balls on the driving range and occasionally shagged balls for members. We made extra money by shining shoes for tips. Occasionally, we would get to caddy for the pro."

He told me that he, too, was a shop boy when he was a lad back in Texas. We talked for a while, and finally, I asked, "Mr. Nelson, it's hard to believe that your stroke average back in 1945 was 68, and you won all those tournaments. The clubs and balls couldn't have been as good as they are today, and you played the same great courses that they still play today. Courses like Merion, Congressional and Pinehurst #2, they couldn't have been in as good a condition back then as they are these days, right?"

He replied, "It's true that the equipment has made great strides in performance and playability over the years, but the golf courses were almost in as good a shape as they are today. To answer your question about my scoring average, I practiced day in and day out for years and would hit hundreds of balls a day. If I wasn't playing golf, I would spend two hours every day working on my short game: chipping, putting, and sand play.

"In 1945, I was playing the best golf of my life. It didn't hurt that my putter was red hot that year, and I did get my fair share of good breaks. I am very proud of the way I played that year." Byron continued, "The game is not just about how well you hit the ball or putt. The most important aspect of the game is mental toughness and understanding and using good course management."

"What is course management?" I asked.

He replied, "Course management is forming a game plan or strategy in your mind about how you plan to play each hole before you start your round. Knowing, beforehand, where to and not to hit the ball is very important to scoring well."

"OK, that makes sense, but what do you do when you are about to play a golf course that you are not familiar with?" I asked.

"That is a very good question, Gaines. The answer is I have the same strategy for every round of golf I play. My goal is to hit the fairways off the tee and hit the greens from the fairway. If you hit the fairway on a par four, you are then playing a par three hole from there. It is much easier to play par threes from the fairway than it is from the rough or from a hazard. I don't hit a driver on every par four. Depending on the hole, I will hit the club that is most likely to give me a good position in the fairway, a two-iron or three-wood, for instance. Accuracy off the tee is more important than distance to me. On par fives, the same is true, except you hit two shots before the hole becomes a par three. When paying my shots on all those par threes, I will, most times, aim for the center of the green. That increases my chances of hitting the green if I miss-hit the shot. If I play the par threes well, I will surely have a good round."

With that, he winked, patted me on the back, shook my hand, and thanked me once again. He stood and, as he was walking away, looked over his shoulder and said, "Good luck with your golfing future, Gaines." That twenty-minute gesture of kindness is an example of why he was known the world over as "Lord Byron."

Courtesy of Ms. Sharron Moran

Chasing A Dream

"Lord Byron Nelson"
Compliments of Greg Alcorn & CC of Salisbury

Chapter 4

Possum Trot Golf Club

It was a Wednesday afternoon in early October 1970, and I was hanging out in the pro shop chatting with our golf pro, Gene Thompson and Ken Alexander, a fellow club member. Ken was a golf and tennis sportswear salesman and covered the Carolinas, calling on every golf and tennis club professional in the two states.

I had graduated five months earlier from Wingate College with a degree in engineering but had yet to decide what I was going to do with my life. While talking with them, I said that I was interested in the possibility of getting a job in the golf business.

"Ken, do you know of any good sales jobs that are open in the golf business that I could apply for?" I asked. "I think I would be a pretty good salesman."

He thought for a moment and replied, "Not right now, Gaines, but if you would be interested in becoming an assistant golf pro, I just might have a great lead for you."

Wow, an assistant golf pro! In my wildest dreams, I hadn't considered getting into the golf business as a professional. The idea, however, intrigued me, so I asked, "Where is the assistant's job located?"

Ken said, "North Myrtle Beach, South Carolina, at a new course called Possum Trot." He had been there two days earlier, and the head pro, Art Joyner, and his wife, Ginny, were looking for an assistant pro to help with the day-to-day operations. The fall golf season on the coast was coming into full swing. Ken gave me Art's contact information and said not to wait too long if I was interested, because Art was sure to fill the position quickly.

I went home to think it over. I hadn't considered moving away from Salisbury. After all, we had only been back home for three years since Seth retired from the Air Force. I needed a job and wasn't excited about the prospect of working for my family in the conveyor manufacturing business. I decided I would give Mr. Joyner a call in the morning.

I awoke excited with the possibility of living and working at the beach. I called Mr. Joiner and talked with him about the job. He asked me when I could come down for an interview. I told him that I could be there the next day around noon.

It was a crisp fall Saturday morning as I headed out toward North Myrtle Beach in my '66 Porsche 911. I had bought the Porsche for $5000.00 from my uncle, who had the first BMW dealership in Charlotte, NC. He sold it to me at a family discount, and I paid for it with money that my grandmother, Kitty, left me when she passed.

The three-and-a-half-hour drive from Salisbury to North Myrtle Beach was indeed picturesque. Two lane state highways were the only routes to take in upstate South Carolina to the beach. From Cheraw eastward, I passed through numerous small historic towns like Clio, Blenheim, Bishopville, Mullins, and Marion, all of them with historic ties to the Revolutionary War.

Marion, South Carolina, was named for Francis Marion, *The Swamp Fox*, a South Carolina officer in the Continental Army. He is credited for inventing the art of modern guerilla warfare.

The speed limit through the center of these small towns was 25 or 30 miles per hour. This offered a wonderful opportunity to take in the beauty of these quaint villages.

Stately mansions lined the main streets. Spanish moss dangled from majestic oak trees on well-manicured lawns. It was like stepping back in time.

Spanish Moss

I arrived at Possum Trot around noon and went inside the clubhouse to meet Mr. and Mrs. Joyner. We exchanged pleasantries and discussed the position while having a bite to eat in the club's snack bar. They asked the routine types of questions one would expect when interviewing for a new position.

The Joyners were originally from Texas and had recently left a golf club in Denver, Colorado, to come to Possum Trot. Art was around fifty years old, and Ginny was eight or so years younger. I liked them right off the bat, and I sensed the feeling was mutual. I excused myself to use the restroom, and upon my return, Art said, "Gaines, we think you would be a good fit with us here. We are willing to offer you the job. When do you think you could start?"

"Well, Mr. Joyner, if I can find a place to stay, I can start tomorrow; my suitcase is in the car," I replied with a wry grin.

They called around to the motels that were associated with the club's golf package and found me a room at the Mustang Motel a few miles down the beach. The rent was $110 a month. It was an efficiency unit with a small oven and refrigerator. I figured that once I got settled into my new job, I would have to find accommodations more suitable for living.

I knew little about the golf history of Myrtle Beach and certainly did not realize that I was about to experience the biggest golfing boom this country has ever seen. Possum Trot had just become the seventeenth course to open in the coastal area known as the Grand Strand. The Grand Strand stretches some 35 miles along the coast of South Carolina, from the Cherry Grove section of North Myrtle Beach southward to Sunset Beach. The area had, for over a century, been a summer playground for beachgoers from all over the eastern United States.

Three years earlier, in 1967, thanks to the visionary genius of several of the area's prominent businessmen, Cecil

Brandon, Gen. Jim Hackler, Clay Brittan and others, Myrtle Beach began a golf explosion like no other. They created the very first golf package promotion, which married hotel rentals with golf tee times in a package deal. They aggressively advertised this promotion in the northeast United States and throughout Canada.

The program was an instant success. Hotels and golf courses started to spring up overnight, and within ten years, the Grand Strand grew from having eleven golf courses to over thirty. The Grand Strand is known today as the "Golfing Capital of The World" and, at one time, had over 100 golf courses with more than 1.5 million rounds of golf played each year! Myrtle Beach golf has two "high" seasons. The fall season runs from late September through late November. The spring season is from mid-February through mid-May.

On my first day of work, I realized that the fall golfing season had arrived. To accommodate more than two hundred players a day, we had to use the double tee system twice a day. The double tee system uses both holes #1 and #10 as starting holes rather than the more common practice of starting all golfers on hole #1. That meant that every 10 minutes, starting at 8:00 a.m., two foursomes, or eight people, would be paying green and cart fees and being directed to their respective starting holes.

Golfers would arrive about thirty minutes before their tee time. At the bag drop area near the front door, they were met by the cart boys, who retrieved their clubs and placed them on the golf carts. After parking their cars, they would come into the pro shop to pay greens fees and cart fees, maybe purchase some golf merchandise or apparel, grab a bite at the snack bar or get a bucket of range balls to warm up with before they tee off.

Occasionally, there were communication mix-ups between hotels and golf courses. Sometimes, the golfers were given the incorrect tee times or even sent to the wrong golf course. These mistakes can cause vacationers to lose their cool and express their disappointment to the golf shop staff. I quickly learned from Art the importance of doing everything possible to resolve these situations with tact and diplomacy. There certainly were hectic times working in the golf shop during the spring and fall high seasons. Art and I did not have any days off. Ginny helped when she could, considering they had two young, school-age daughters to raise.

A month after my arrival at Possum Trot, Art, and Ginny hired a second assistant pro, Leonard Thompson, from Lumberton, North Carolina. Leonard had a very successful amateur golfing resume. He had recently graduated from Wake Forest University, where he was a starter on the golf team. The Wake Forest Demon Deacons were one of the nation's highest-ranked golf teams, year after year. It is the alma mater of many of the tour's finest players, including Arnold Palmer.

Leonard and I worked well together, and we had the opportunity to take one day off per week. As the season started to wind down, Art devised a schedule for Leonard and me that enabled us to enjoy the fruits of our labor. Every other day, Art and I would go in early to open and handle the morning flow of golfers. At eleven-thirty, Leonard would arrive, and he and I would overlap our time in the shop until one o'clock. I then had the afternoon off while Leonard stayed until closing time. The next day, we would flip the schedule. Leonard would open and I would stay 'til closing time. This schedule worked well for me and Leonard, and great for Art. He loved the game with passion and would play every afternoon if the opportunity presented itself. On my afternoons off, Art and I would play golf together.

Art was an accomplished instructor and improved my game immensely. Some afternoons, we would go to other golf courses in the area and play a money match with that club's pro and his assistant. That was my introduction to gambling on the golf course. On the other afternoons, Art and Leonard would venture off to do the same thing. Art was in hog heaven, playing nearly every day accompanied by his two sidekicks.

Leonard Thompson   Art Joyner   Gaines Beard

Chasing A Dream

With the work schedule affording me some time off, it was time to start looking for a more appropriate place to live. On the corner of the street leading into Possum Trot was the Crescent Beach Post Office, which I frequented nearly every day, picking up the mail on my way to work. Herbert White, the postmaster, and I had become friends. I knew that if there was a place to rent in North Myrtle Beach, he would know about it.

One day, I asked, "Mr. White, do you know of any apartments or efficiencies for rent here in Crescent Beach?"

He said, "Gaines, I know of several nice places not far from here, but I don't know if any of them are available. Let me ask around, and tomorrow, I will let you know what I find out."

The next afternoon, around two o'clock, instead of playing golf, I headed straight to the post office. Mr. White was smiling as I entered the glass front door.

"Well, did you find an apartment that is available for rent?"

Mr. White, still smiling, said, "I'll give you one better than that. Do you know the Baldwin Company Hardware Store, on Main Street?"

"Sure," I replied, "you can find almost anything you are looking for in there. The place is huge!"

He said, "Mrs. Baldwin is a widow and getting on in age. Her home is just five blocks away, down 17th Avenue, and just one block off the ocean. Behind her home, in a huge backyard, is the quaintest little cottage you have ever seen. I told her that you seemed to be a fine young man, so she told me to have you give her a call."

I was very excited to hear this news and thanked Mr. White profusely. I went straight to the pay phone outside the entrance of the post office and called Mrs. Baldwin. I introduced myself and asked when I might be able to come by to see her cottage. She said to stop by the next afternoon after four o'clock.

I was amazed that everything had happened so quickly and was looking forward to meeting Mrs. Baldwin. I knew that I should display my best southern charm, as I was not only looking at her cottage, but she would be checking me out as well.

Mrs. Baldwin was a lovely lady in her sixties. It was clear that she and her husband had been very successful. She was wearing a navy-blue dress and a beautiful string of pearls. Her gray hair was in a bun, and there was a welcoming glint in her eyes. She invited me into the parlor, where we enjoyed a cup of tea served on a silver tray with fine chinaware.

We chatted for a while before going around to look at the cottage. I assured her that I was not the rowdy sort and would not play my music too loud and cause a ruckus.

The cottage was lovelier than I had expected. It was painted white with dark green shutters. It sat amid three huge Spanish moss-ladened oak trees that kept it in the shade throughout the day. It was nicely furnished and had a living room-kitchen area, a bathroom, and a bedroom. It was perfect. She agreed to rent it to me for a hundred and fifty dollars a month, utilities included, for as long as I wanted.

With summer just months away, I knew it would not be long before the beach, just one block away, would be teeming with young ladies on spring break. I found myself living a fairy tale existence. I was twenty-one years old, had a wonderful job, an impressive sports car, and lived in a beautiful cottage just blocks from the beach. The only thing missing was a girlfriend. I figured a surefire way to attract a young lady was to go out and

Chasing A Dream

buy myself an adorable little puppy to go with me on my "trolls" along the beach.

Chapter 5

Mrs. Baldwin's Cottage

At the time, I didn't know a lot about dog breeds. We only had three dogs while I was growing up. The first was a German Shepherd that my father bought from a breeder twelve weeks after I was born. My mother named her Cosima, which came from the feminine Greek name meaning "order." Mom considered herself a student of ancient history.

My father thought it would be funny to have a dog that was born on the same day I was. Cosima and I would celebrate our birthdays together, eating ice cream and cake. She would sit in a chair at the head of the table with me, my older brother

Bryce, and our cousin Cam. Cosima was a large dog, and when we were four, she bit me in the face, sending me to the emergency room for stitches. From that day forward, I steered clear of all German Shepherds.

Our second dog was a mongrel named Beau. Seth and Mom found him at a dog shelter in Columbus, Ohio, when I was eight. Beau was a loveable little guy who looked somewhat like a miniature Collie. He was playful, obedient and a constant companion. As a child, having Beau gave me my love and admiration for dogs.

The last dog of my childhood was a full-blooded Weimaraner named Schatzi. My mother named her, too. We lived in Cheyenne, Wyoming and got Schatzi when I was fourteen. She was short-haired, muscular, and had a shiny grey coat and a cropped tail. Schatzi was my mother's and became a house dog. She was a sweet dog but a little high-strung for my mother. After about a year, Seth gave Schatzi to a fellow officer who had three young children and a fenced-in backyard.

I was determined to get a puppy before schools let out for spring break. I had not given much thought to the responsibilities of dog ownership. I asked Mrs. Baldwin's permission to get one, and she agreed with the following stipulations: The dog was not to damage the cottage's furniture or carpet and it was not to bother her or her neighbors with unnecessary barking.

Being young and naïve, these requests seemed simple enough. I didn't know what breed of dog I wanted. All puppies are cute, but I wanted a dog that would be cute, even as it got older. I started looking in the newspaper classifieds for puppies for sale or adoption. Within a few weeks, I spotted an ad for Irish Setter puppies. I knew they were beautiful bird dogs with flowing auburn hair and were natural pointers. As if frozen in time, it was indeed a sight to see a bird dog go on point. It would stand in place, eyes fixed forward, unwavering, with a front paw lifted and the two hind legs in a pouncing stance. Its tail, with a shimmering red mane, stood straight out and erect.

The ad stated that they were full-blooded but without AKC registered papers. At seventy-five dollars each, they were practically giving them away, considering the family had taken the puppies to the veterinarian for checkups and shots.

I arranged to pick up my new beach walking partner the following Saturday. On my way there, I stopped by a pet store for supplies, canned dog food, a bowl, a dog bed, a collar, a leash, treats, and various dog toys.

I had my choice between two remaining puppies out of a litter of six, one male and one female. They were equally beautiful and playful, so the decision was difficult. I thought for a moment that I might go "eenie, meenie, miny, moe." But instead, I used simple reasoning. Since we were going to troll the beach looking for girls, I should get the boy dog. It made perfect sense to me at the time. It wasn't long before I realized that I may have made the wrong decision.

On the drive back to North Myrtle Beach, with my new, adorable, wide-eyed friend sitting next to me, I needed to come up with an appropriate name for such a stately animal. His name would stick with him forever. I should give this matter serious consideration and was NOT going to ask my mother for suggestions.

We arrived home shortly before dark. I took my puppy and his treasure trove of goodies inside to settle in for the night. He ate from his new bowl, and I couldn't wait to take him for a walk around the backyard. To my delight, after only a few minutes of sniffing and tugging at the leash, he did his business, both numbers one and two. The backyard was mostly sand, so it was easy to bury the evidence. Surely, house training was going to be easier than I had imagined.

I spent the rest of the evening playing with him and holding him on my lap. He seemed happy in his new surroundings and explored every inch of his new home. He tried to lie down and nap a few times, but I was having none of that. I wanted to keep him up as late as possible. I figured that way, he might sleep through the night.

At ten o'clock, I put him in the kitchen on the linoleum floor, with a water bowl and his new comfy bed. I barricaded the kitchen off with moving boxes to keep him in the kitchen.

I watched a little TV while hardly taking my eyes off the little fella'. Before long, he curled up on his bed next to a stuffed teddy bear and went to sleep. I fell asleep on the sofa, adoring my beautiful little puppy. At four in the morning, I was awakened by screeching yelps. His vocal cords were not developed enough to produce real barking. I picked him up and we cuddled for a while on the sofa. It hit me that I should take him outside to go potty again. In no time, he squatted and tee-teed once more. I was beside myself at how smart he seemed to be.

We retired, and in the morning, I had to go to work. In an instant, it became abundantly clear that I had not given adequate study to the responsibilities of owning a pet and working at the same time. Hurriedly, I took him out to do his business, but to no avail. We returned to his nest in the kitchen, covered the floor with newspapers and left him with some food and fresh water. I would come home around noon to check on him.

Upon my return, I saw that he had done his complete business several times on the newspapers and had torn an ear off his teddy bear. I cleaned up the mess, put down fresh newspapers and refilled his water bowl. We went outside for a walk and noticed Mrs. Baldwin descending her back steps.

"Good afternoon, Gaines. What do you have there?" I picked up my puppy and walked over to Mrs. Baldwin.

"This is my new puppy. I picked him up yesterday afternoon. Isn't he cute?"

"Oh my, he is adorable. What have you named him?" I was immediately embarrassed that I had not given him a name, and in a split second, I felt my mouth open and blurt out, "Rhett Butler, I named him Rhett Butler."

"That is a marvelous name for such a lovely boy. I hope he doesn't cause you too much trouble during his puppy stage."

"So far, so good," I said, "but I'm going to keep my fingers crossed." She smiled, said goodbye, then turned and walked toward her big, black Lincoln Continental.

I took Rhett back inside and marveled at my quick thinking. Rhett Butler was a good name, I thought, and very southern. I was sure my mother would approve.

The Holiday Inn North was a six-story oceanfront hotel located just three blocks down the beach from my cottage. On the ground floor, just off the lobby, was the Beachcomber Lounge, a dimly lit, smoke-filled mecca for cocktails, live music, and dancing. It was the place to party after dark with a revolving door of young ladies throughout the summer. I spent a lot of evenings there.

On my afternoons off, Rhett and I would stroll those three blocks to the beach behind the Holiday Inn North. It was indeed a target-rich environment, teeming with young college-age girls looking to have a little fun. It had a large swimming pool with a swim-up tiki bar. That is where Rhett and I would hang out because it offered a constant stream of thirsty vacationers and a perfect place for "breaking the ice" small talk.

Rhett's cuteness was hard to ignore. You would be surprised at how often a young lady would pause by my table in the Beachcomber Lounge and say, "Didn't I see you at the beach this afternoon with a cute little puppy?"

"You must have," I said, "he loves to walk the beach and frolic in the shallows."

"He's adorable," she would say. "What is his name?"

I would reply, "Rhett Butler," with a big grin on my face. All the girls loved Rhett Butler, both the southern gentleman in *Gone With The Wind* and my Irish Setter puppy.

Gaines Beard

I had a summer at the beach that most boys could never dream of. I met some lovely girls and fell in love a couple of times. Long-distance relationships are difficult at a young age, and frankly, at twenty-one, what did I really know about love?

I did, however, meet a young girl that summer that was virtually impossible to forget. One afternoon, Rhett and I were walking on the beach and encountered a group of teenagers sunbathing behind a beach house near the Holiday Inn. One of them jumped up and came over to pet Rhett. She looked to be about fifteen. She was a stunningly beautiful young girl with an incredible smile and long blonde hair. She offered the normal petting and adoration Rhett had become accustomed to.

After a moment, I asked, "Where are you girls from?"

"We live here in Cresent Beach."

"Really?" I said. "You are a native?"

"Yes, sir, I sure am. My daddy is the postmaster here, and we all go to Horry County Middle School."

"Herb White is your father?" I asked.

"Yes," she replied. "Do you know him?" I went on to tell her that I was an assistant pro at Possum Trot Golf Club, and Herb was our postmaster. I told her that her father even found me Mrs. Baldwin's cottage to rent.

"That's cool, Mrs. Baldwin is a nice lady. See you later."

See you later, indeed she would. A year and a half later, I was married with a new baby. Occasionally, we would need a babysitter. Herb said that his daughter babysat, and it worked out that she was our regular babysitter, especially on weeknights.

On one occasion, she could not babysit for us even though it was a Monday night. It was my twenty-forth birthday, February 18, 1974. It just so happened to be her birthday, too.

I can't help but remember this lovely girl to this day. She graduated college, did some modeling in Georgia then moved to California to follow her dreams. She found her fame turning letters on "The Wheel of Fortune."

Yes, Vanna White was Herb White's daughter.

Chapter 6

Dreadful News

There are certain events that occur during your lifetime that you remember exactly where you were and what you were doing when you learned about them. For example, the day that President John F. Kennedy was assassinated in Dallas, Texas.

It was late in the morning of November 22, 1963, and I was at my grandparents' home in Salisbury, North Carolina, recuperating from a tonsillectomy. I was sitting in front of their Zenith console TV, playing with my grandfather's tape-recording machine. It was one of the first of its kind, manufactured by Timex, the wristwatch company often advertised by John Cameron Swayze. He coined the slogan, "It takes a licking and keeps on ticking." The tape-recording machine was heavy for its size, three inches high and ten inches square. It resembled a record player. It had an arm with a needle at the end that rested on a thin, floppy plastic disc that resembled a 45 record. A microphone was attached to it with a braided fabric cord.

I was watching a morning game show when the large CBS eye logo covered the screen, and I heard, "We interrupt this program to bring you breaking news. Here is Walter Cronkite."

"John F. Kennedy, the 35th president of the United States, was shot at 12:30 p.m. Central Standard Time while riding in a presidential motorcade through Dealey Plaza in Dallas, Texas. Kennedy was in the vehicle with his wife, Jacqueline, Texas Governor John Connally, and Connally's wife, Nellie."

Understandably shocked, I decided to press the record button on the Timex and recorded until CBS resumed its regular scheduled program. I knew my grandparents would want to hear this horrible news if they hadn't heard it already.

It was the morning of September 11, 2001, just before nine o'clock. I was in the kitchen of my condominium at Lake Norman, NC, making breakfast before starting my workday. The telephone rang, and my next-door neighbor said, "Are you watching the news? Turn it on right now." And he hung up.

Like everyone else in the country, for the next three hours, I was in total shock and disbelief at what I was hearing and seeing. Two commercial airliners were crashing into the top floors of The World Trade Center in New York City. It was the most horrific live television imaginable, and at the time, we really had no concrete information about what was happening.

The date was November 11, 1972. I was busy in the pro shop at Possum Trot, checking in golfers and manning the cash register. The phone rang and Art, my boss, answered it in his office. A moment later, Art appeared and told me that I had a call and should take it in his office.

I picked up the receiver. "Hello," I said. It was my brother Bryce on the other end. I will never forget the first two words out of his mouth. "Daddy's dead!"

I didn't comprehend his words at first. Listening in shock, Bryce told me that our father, an alcoholic, had been taken to

Wilmoth Hospital in Charlotte for a ten-day sobriety or "drying out" period.

Wilmoth was not a hospital in the pure sense of the word. You would not go there for medical treatments for illnesses, accidents, broken bones, etc. Wilmoth was a private institution that catered to those who suffered from drug and alcohol addictions. It was a place of a dozen or so rooms with a doctor and nurse on call. Orderlies did most of the day-to-day chores, and many of them were recovering alcoholics themselves, who would work off their debt from one of their previous stays. My father had been a "patient" there a handful of times through the years.

"They found him dead in his room this morning," Bryce said. "You need to come back to Salisbury to help with the arrangements."

I hung up the phone and sat for what seemed like an eternity. Many thoughts raced through my mind. When was the last time I called him just to say hello or dropped by to pay him a visit when I was in town? Did he know that I loved him deeply and understood his illness without judgment? Had I shown him the respect he deserved? Did I ever tell him that I loved him?

Shock, sadness, and guilt are strange bedfellows. I came out of the office and could instantly tell that Art and Ginny knew about my father's passing. Ginny gave me a big hug. Art put his hand on my shoulders, looked me square in the eyes and said, "Gaines, is there anything we can do?"

I looked up at Art, and with tears in my eyes, "I don't have anything to wear to my father's funeral."

The next morning, I was heading home. That four-hour drive home was painful. Thoughts raced through my mind about the times I spent with my father. The times he would take me and my brother to the club pool to swim when he got off work. He taught me to swim when I was barely four years old. When I was five, he taught me to ride a bicycle.

He would often take us to the Center Theatre located in a building that my grandfather owned. At that young age, I still remember how special I felt going to the movies and never having to pay to get in.

We left Salisbury when I was seven with our stepfather, who was in the Air Force. I rarely got to see my father for the next ten years until we moved back home when Seth retired from the service.

***

My father, Bryce Parker Beard, Jr., was the oldest of four boys. When my father and his brothers reached high school age, they did not attend the local high school. My grandfather enrolled each one of them in The Georgia Military Academy in Atlanta. For twelve years, one and sometimes two of the Beard boys would board the Southern Crescent train bound for Atlanta with trips home only for Christmas and summer vacations. It was required of them to join the military upon graduation. College would have to wait.

Dad joined the Marine Corps and went off to fight the Japanese in the Pacific Theater. He was at Guadalcanal and Iwo Jima and was awarded the Bronze Star for valor. When the war was over, he returned home to Salisbury, a different man with his own private demons.

He entered the University of North Carolina to study Art and Literature. Alcohol had found its way into my father's misery. It wasn't long before he was known on campus as "Dr. Beard" because he carried a medical bag filled with rye and gin.

For the rest of his life, he struggled with the disease, as did so many other young servicemen who suffered from Post Traumatic Stress Disorder as it is known today.

I returned home to help my brother and uncles clean out my father's apartment and sort through his outstanding obligations. Three days later, he was buried at C

Chestnut Hill Cemetery, next to his father and mother and not far from the pink granite Beard mausoleum that entombed his grandparents.

Grandson Parker Beard

A week later, I returned to N. Myrtle Beach and my assistant pro job. The next day, Art reminded me that the Carolina's Assistant Pro Championship would be held at the Pine Lakes International Country Club just twenty miles down the coast. It was to start in five days. I had entered the tournament three weeks earlier but had not thought about it in a week. It had completely slipped my mind.

"I don't know, Art," I said. "With all that has been happening lately and this November being so busy with tourists, I don't think I'm ready to play in a major championship. I've only played three rounds in the past month."

"Horseshit!" Art shouted, "Your game is in good shape; you're only a little rusty. I'll give you plenty of time to practice this week. You have the game, and it will be good for you to take your mind off your sadness for a while."

Over the next four days, I practiced a lot. I went to work an hour early to concentrate on my short game: chipping, sand shots, and putting. It was chilly in the mornings, the best time to practice the short game because the muscles and joints weren't ready for full-throttle ball striking. I would hit balls on the range during lunch and after work. I'd play golf until it got dark and continued playing by feel until I lost the ball. Playing golf at night is great practice, so long as you don't drive the cart into a pond.

***

For the first round of the thirty-six-hole championship, I had an 8:20 a.m. tee time. I got up early, showered and shaved, had a cup of coffee, and headed straight to the range at Possum

Trot. It wasn't for short game practice that morning. It was time to ready myself for eighteen holes of golf with a singular purpose and eagle-eye concentration. I hit a bucket of balls and loosened my muscles. After the short drive to Pine Lakes, I proceeded straight to the putting green to practice on their greens.

I was shocked to find that they had, two weeks earlier, reseeded their greens with winter rye grass. The grass was too young and delicate to mow; therefore, the soft blades were three-quarters of an inch long. I knew that putts would not break as much as usual, and the greens would be extremely slow.

Putting becomes more of a hitting or popping stroke rather than the usual smooth stroke used on regular mature greens where the blades of grass are less than a quarter of an inch long.

That morning, it was colder than normal. You could see your breath when you exhaled. There had been a thirty-minute frost delay, so my tee time was pushed back to 8:50. That suited me just fine; let it warm up.

I was dressed in corduroy slacks and layered in a short sleeve t-shirt, long sleeve t-shirt, long sleeve turtleneck, and a sweater. I wore a toboggan knit hat and golf gloves on both hands. I had a hand warmer and wore a rainsuit over my clothing to cut the wind and hold my body heat in. I admit I felt like I was the Pillsbury Doughboy.

Two other pros and I teed off together, and from the start, I was making good contact with the ball by slowing down my swing due to the clothing restrictions.

On the first nine holes, I made six pars, two bogies and one birdie for a one over 36. I played well on the back nine except for two "yipped" putts."

With a first round of 74, I found myself tied for second place with Sam Marsh of Boone, NC and one stroke back of Russell Glover of Summerville, S.C. I rushed back to Possum Trot to give Art and Ginny the good news. I was beside myself with joy and pride. Yes, I was proud of myself for showing that my four days of practice had paid off.

I was paired with Sam and Russell for the second round, with a tee time at 10:12 a.m. We were the last group to go off. It was a terrific opportunity to be in the final threesome with the other two frontrunners. I liked knowing where I stood in a tournament, and that day, I would know firsthand.

We all played well, trading shot for shot, with no one opening more than a two-stroke advantage on the front nine. As we made the turn, I spotted Art with Tommy Heywood, the head pro at Beechwood Golf Club next door to Possum Trot. The fact that they had taken the time to come and watch me play my final nine holes meant the world to me.

When we arrived at the sixteenth tee, I was one stroke back of Russell and tied with Sam with three holes to play. Sam and I both birdied sixteen while Russel parred, making the three of us tied with two to go. I birdied the seventeenth to take a one-stroke advantage going into the final hole. This is when I let my guard down and had a lapse in concentration. Instead of staying in the moment, with clear focus of "one shot at a time," my mind began to wander.

The mind can go anywhere in an instant. I saw myself in first place, and I couldn't help from seeing the headlines about the local pro who won the championship by birding two of the last three holes a week after burying his father. I am sure that lack of focus and placing myself ahead of things cost me dearly.

I bogeyed the eighteenth, and Randy, Sam and I all finished with a two-day total of 144. We congratulated each other, figuring we would meet again at the first tee for a sudden-death playoff. When we entered the scorer's tent and saw the scoreboard, our hopes were dashed. Larry Beck of Whispering Pines N.C. fired a final round of 70 to finish in first place with 143.

I learned that day that the phrase "DON'T TAKE YOUR EYES OFF THE BALL" had more than one meaning.

Art, Ginny, and I celebrated that night over dinner and drinks at the Embers Steakhouse, our local haunt. I was still very proud of myself after all the dust settled. I'd like to think that my father was too.

Courtesy of The Salisbury Post

*A yip is a term to describe the involuntary, uncontrollable spasm that a golfer occasionally gets in his hands and wrists when stroking the putt. It is an electrical-like twitch that causes uncontrolled muscle movements that guarantee a missed putt. It is the worst feeling in golf.

Chasing A Dream

Possum Trot Pro Comes In Second

By TOM HUNTER

Gaines Beard had his figures right but his course of aim was slightly wrong in last week's 17th annual Carolina PGA Section Championship for Assistant Professionals.

The 22-year-old assistant professional at Possum Trot Golf Club in North Myrtle Beach was playing in the same foursome as first day leader Russell Glover of Summerville. Beard figured he had to birdie the par five final hole to be in a position to win the event which was held at the Pine Lakes International Country Club in Myrtle Beach, the Grand Strand's oldest course.

He figured right, but his eight-foot putt for a birdie lipped the cup and the Salisbury, N.C., native found himself one shot back of the winner Avery Beck of Whispering Pines, N.C.

The shot that really cost him the chance to win, however, was his approach shot to the green which fell short and landed in a sand trap.

"On the last hole I drove down the right side on the edge of the fairway," Gaines said as he thought back over the tournament. "I had about 180 yards to the green and the ball was sitting up on some high grass.

"I figured the ball would fly on me and my adrenaline was really flowing, so I hit a five-iron rather than a four. I ended up in a sand trap on the right."

"I hit what I thought was a good sand shot eight feet short of the hole. I figured I had to make the putt. It had a foot and a half break to the right and it lipped it out."

Glover had about a 12-foot putt for a birdie and also figured he had to make the putt to win. He sank the putt but still finished one shot back of the leader.

The victory for Beck marked the third time he has won the tournament. Beck, who is an assistant pro to his father and was formerly a professional at Beachwood Golf Course at North Myrtle Beach when it started four years ago, also won the event in 1961 and 1962.

Beard had a 37-36-73 on the first day of the tournament and was in a tie for third. Glover's opening day 69 was the low score for the event over the par 71, 6,609-yard course.

On the second day, Beard bogied the birst two holes and finished his first nine holes two shots over par. Playing the front side last, he birdied seven and eight but could only manage par on the 470-yard par five ninth hole.

Beard said it was a "funny experience waiting all year for the tournament and then you have only one chance the whole year."

first day and 33 putts the second and both days I had three-putt greens."

Beard said the entire course was in good shape, and added: "I'm appreciative to the members who gave up the course for a couple of days. They've done this eight years in a row when this tournament comes around.

"I'm pleased I played as well as I can under the circumstances and I'm looking forward to playing again next year."

Beard, who has been at Possum Trot for two and one-half years, is now looking toward the South Carolina Chapter Pro-Am in Columbia Dec. 11-12 at Spring Valley.

Beck received $500 for winning the tournament which carried a $4,000 purse and the second place finishers each received $266.63.

SCORES

1. Larry Beck, Whispering Pines, N.C. — 73-72 — 145, $500.
2. Gaines Bard, North Myrtle Beach, S.C. — 73-73 — 146, $266; Russell Glover, Summerville, S.C. — 69-77 — 146, $266; Sam Marsh, Aiken, S.C. — 73-73 — 146, $266.
3. Ray Perry, Fayetteville, N.C. — 74-76 — 150, $140; Tom Bailey, Charlotte, N.C. — 74-76 — 150, $140.
4. Jeff Howell, Charleston, S.C. — 78-73 — 151, $100; Johnny Briggs, Winston Salem, N.C. — 73-78 — 151, $100; David Robinson, Burlington, N.C. — 75-76 — 151, $100.
5. Earl Pruet, Columbia, S.C. — 73-79 — 152, $75; Mike Hamilton, Fountain Inn, S.C. — 76-76 — 152, $75.

Courtesy The Sun News

Chapter 7

Starting A Family

It was late January in 1972, just after twelve noon, when our greens superintendent, Donny Christenberry, walked into the pro shop to take his lunch break. Instead of heading directly to the snack bar, he came over to the golf counter, where I was perched on a stool reading Golf Digest. He said, "Gaines, a new golf course just opened on the other side of Beechwood. It's called Azalea Sands, and it is going to be a great track. There is a cute young shop girl working there that I know. She was one of my lifeguards last year when I ran the beach lifeguard services here in North Myrtle Beach. Her name is Gracie, and if I were you, I would go over there as soon as I could and meet her."

"Really?" I asked. "Do you know where she is from?"

"Yep, she's from Columbia and living down here full-time."

I wasn't dating anyone at that time and being partial to southern belles, decided to go by Azalea Sands the next afternoon and look for myself.

The next morning, I was anxious about the prospect of meeting Gracie. I wanted to make a good impression, so I put on my best golf outfit and my favorite shoes: FootJoy alligator street shoes.

That morning, the minute hand on the clock seemed to move in slow motion like it had molasses on it. Finally, it was noon, and I told Art, "I am going over to Azalea Sands to check out the shop girl that Donny told me about yesterday. He said she was really cute."

"So that's it," Art said, "I wondered why you were wearing your prized gators to work." Smiling, he said, "Good luck, son; I can't wait to hear all about it."

I hopped into my Porsche and drove a quarter mile to Azalea Sands. When I entered the pro shop, there was, indeed, a beautiful young gal standing behind the counter. I almost tripped on the welcome mat, not watching where I was going. She must have a boyfriend, I thought, as I caught my balance before completely embarrassing myself. She had shoulder-length dirty blonde hair and wore a short light purple sun dress that was dotted with yellow smiley faces. Before I could mosey over to make my certain-to-be nervous introduction, a friend of mine called out to me from the other side of the room.

"Hey, pro, come over here and tell me what you think of this putter."

Man, what perfect timing! I knew Gracie heard him call me pro, and I got a chance to do my "pro stuff," sensing she was watching from across the room. After a few minutes strutting around like a peacock, I told my pal that I would see him later.

I turned and walked straight over to the counter and, looking straight into her eyes, said, "You must be Gracie."

I wish you could have seen the look on her face. She had a look of surprise as she replied, "Yes, how did you know that?"

"I am an assistant pro at Possum Trot, and Donny Christenberry is our greenskeeper. He told me to come over here and meet you. My name is Gaines Beard."

"It's nice to meet you," she said as she extended her hand.

We exchanged small talk for a few minutes then I asked her when her lunch break was. She said her roommate, Nettie Bates, was coming to have lunch with her in the snack bar and asked me if I would like to join them.

"Sounds great," I said. I excused myself and went to the snack bar and ordered myself a beer and sat down at a corner table.

Soon, Gracie and Nettie entered the room. I stood and introduced myself to Nettie while removing my hat. We sat down, ordered sandwiches, and chatted like old friends. It turned out that Nettie was ten years older than we were and was a nurse at the local hospital, Ocean View Memorial.

I finally got up the nerve and said, "Gracie, would you like to have dinner with me tonight at the Embers Steakhouse?"

"Well, I'm not…"

"Why don't you have dinner with Gaines tonight?" Nettie butted in. "He seems like a nice young man, and you don't have any other plans, do you?"

Gracie looked at me shyly and said, "No, not really. I guess it would be OK."

It was set; I was going on my first date in months with a beautiful and fun girl from Columbia, South Carolina. The plan was to pick her up at Nettie's at seven o'clock. I was beside myself as I drove back to Possum Trot to tell Art all about it. Art was happy for me and handed me a twenty-dollar bill and said, "Here, take this. I want you to show her a good time without worrying about the money. After all, first impressions are very important."

I drove to Nettie's at seven and rang the doorbell. Nettie asked me in and said Gracie was almost ready. It was then that I sensed Nettie was in her big sister's protection mode. She said, "Gaines, I am sure you are going to behave yourself tonight. I want you to have Gracie home by eleven. She has work tomorrow."

"Don't worry, Nettie. I like Gracie and will try my best to make a good impression. I will have her home by eleven."

Gracie appeared from her room looking even more beautiful than earlier that day. Her hair had flip curls, and she wore a gorgeous pink sundress with open-toed white sandals. Her fingernails and toenails were a soft shade of red. She was stunning. It was obvious to me that she wanted to make a good impression on me as well.

The Embers was a dimly lit nightclub with candles on linen tablecloths. They had live music nightly and were known for their fine steaks and seafood. It was on the corner at the entrance to Possum Trot, and it was owned by one of Possum Trot's co-owners. Art, Ginny, and I frequented it often and knew the staff by name.

Gracie seemed impressed when the hostess, waiter, and bartender all said something like, "It's good to see you again, Gaines," or "Are you going to have the usual, Mr. Beard?"

We had a lovely evening dining, dancing, and talking like old friends. We were both Episcopalians and had a lot in common. I got Gracie home by ten forty-five, opened her car door, walked her to the porch, kissed her and said, "Gracie, I had a great time tonight. Would you like to go out tomorrow?"

"I had a wonderful time, too, Gaines. Sure, I'll go out with you again."

That is how it started. It may sound like a cliché, but it was truly love at first sight. I called my mother first thing the next morning with the news of my infatuation with Gracie Hopkins. Right off the bat, she wanted to know, "Where is she from, and who are her people?"

I told Mom that she was from Columbia and an Episcopalian. I told her that I thought she might be the one. That afternoon, my mother called her Aunt Julia Fisher, a lifelong Columbian and woman with social standing. As fate would have it, Julia told my mother, "Mary Marshall, I know Gracie's parents. In fact, her mother, Frances, is in my book club, and she is a lovely lady. The Hopkins family is old in South Carolina. There is a township just east of Columbia named Hopkins, South Carolina, after her family. Years ago, they had one of the largest plantations in central South Carolina."

Aunt Julia went on to tell my mother that Gracie was a debutante and had graduated from the University of South Carolina. My mother called me later that afternoon and relayed to me what Julia had told her. She said, "Gaines, you have my permission to marry her." Gracie had my mother's seal of approval.

Two weeks later, after an evening dancing under the stars at the Pad Beach Bar, I got down on one knee and, with a ring that belonged to my grandmother, Kitty, asked Gracie to marry me. She said yes, and three months later, on May 13, 1972, we were married at Saint Martin's in the Fields Episcopal Church in Columbia, South Carolina. Talk about a spring romance!

We got married earlier than we originally planned because I was accepting a new assistant pro position in Panama City Beach, Florida, in mid-May.

The morning after the wedding, Gracie and I headed out to Panama City Beach. Around six p.m., we pulled into a Day's Inn in Cordele, GA. The motel was new, and there was a Putt-Putt of America right next door. We played mini-golf at the Putt-Putt while enjoying chili dogs and a couple of Miller Lites. Little did I know how fortunate that putting practice was going to be when we got to Panama City the next day.

We arrived at the pro shop's temporary trailer around 10 a.m. the next morning. Howell Frazier, whom I had caddied for in the Kemper Open in Charlotte when I was nineteen, greeted us with open arms.

"Gaines and Gracie, I am so glad to see y'all. Welcome! How was the wedding and the trip down?"

I went on to detail the high points of the ceremony and told him we stopped off the previous night in Dothan and played miniature golf.

"That's great!" He chuckled. "I'm glad to hear you got in some putting practice because today you are going to need it."

"Oh, really... Why's that?"

"We're going over to the Panama City Country Club, my home course, and play the head pro there and a local guy trying to make the tour. I want to introduce you to them."

"That is great, Howell, I can't wait."

We chatted a while, and Gracie got suggestions for sightseeing, which she wanted to do before we checked in to our hotel later that evening.

Howell and I drove over to the country club and Gracie was to pick me up around six back at the trailer. He introduced me to the head professional and the aspiring tour pro, Jim Chancey. We exchanged pleasantries and proceeded to the practice tee to warm up before teeing off at one o'clock.

Early in the round, I was putting like a man possessed! I one-putted twice in the first three holes. Chancey commented to me as we left the third green, "Do you make everything you look at?"

"No," I chuckled. "It's probably because last night my bride and I played mini-golf on our way down here, and these greens are about the same speed as those at the Putt-Putt."

"Putt-Putt..." Jim laughed. "Damn, I'm going to have to try that."

I played great that afternoon. I don't remember many details after the third hole, but there is one thing that I will never forget. I shot 64 that day, the lowest round of my life. Howell had a 65, and Jim and his partner both shot 69. Howell and I field-stripped them out of a hundred and twenty-five dollars. That was a week's pay for an assistant pro. What a start to my new position!

I didn't realize it at the time, but my beating Howell, who was fresh off the tour in front of his two buddies, didn't sit too well with him. I could sense a slight chill towards me from that day forward. It never crossed my mind not to show up my boss right out of the gate. In my defense, I never dreamed I would play that well.

That week, Gracie and I bought a new twelve-hundred-square-foot brick slab home just three blocks off the Gulf Shore. We were very lucky to find that house. It was owned by a local contractor who built and furnished it for his daughter. For reasons unknown, she never moved into the house.

What a stroke of luck to find a new, fully furnished house in a great new subdivision for a price we could afford, $18,500.00. It was a cute little house, with a living area open through a breakfast area to the kitchen. On the left side of the house were two small bedrooms with an adjoining bathroom. The laundry room was located at the rear of the carport. It was perfect; however, I could have done without the green shag carpet covering every floor in the house.

One of the members of the club gave Gracie a job swimming with dolphins at his amusement facility, Gulf World. We both loved Panama City Beach. The sugar-white sand beach was just a short walk from our house. I stayed in contact with Art throughout the summer. I had left him at the end of the spring season, so he didn't have to hire an assistant to replace me until October.

***

In late September, Art and I were talking on the phone. He asked me if I was happy in my new job, and I told him that it wasn't working out as I had hoped it would.

"Gaines," he said, "If you aren't happy there, Ginny and I could sure use you in a month or so."

"Really, Art?" I replied. "Let me think about it, and I will get back to you."

Art said, "I believe you know where you belong now."

After my conversation with Art, Gracie and I discussed our situation. She really wanted to be closer to her family, so we contacted a realtor about our house. We were told that it would be no problem getting our money back out of the house, so a week after talking with Art, Gracie and I headed back home to North Myrtle Beach.

We found a large apartment above the World Carpet Center, not far from Possum Trot on Highway 17. A friend of Art's, Harry Thomas, offered Gracie a job as a sales associate in his store, The Beach Shop on Main Street in Ocean Drive Beach. Things were now back to normal again and we loved being back home in the Carolinas.

One Saturday in early February, we awoke to one of the rarest events ever to happen at Myrtle Beach. There were three inches of snow on our deck, and there didn't seem to be any letup in sight. I got dressed and went to the store to buy bacon, eggs, milk, bread, and toilet paper, just like everyone else.

That afternoon, we watched old black and white movies and marveled at the magical white, snowy wonderland outside our windows. Around 6:30 that evening, the power went out. We had not eaten yet, so I called around local restaurants to see if any of them were open. Luckily, Antonio's Italian Restaurant, a local hangout, was open and had power and entertainment.

We dressed warmly and carefully descended the twenty snow-covered steel steps down to the parking lot. After warming up our 63' Chevy and scraping the windshield, we headed out for Antonio's, some five miles up Highway 17. Snowflakes the size of dimes were falling heavily. It was at least six inches thick on the road, which was deserted except for us.

It took nearly twenty-five minutes to reach the restaurant. There were only fifteen cars in the parking lot that we could make out through the thick blizzard.

We were well-known at Antonio's and were treated like family. Antonio greeted us and said that they were only serving one entre that night, lasagna. That suited us just fine as he showed us to a small table in the lounge. On stage was a piano player and friend of ours, Vernon Suthe. Singing with him was my golf pro buddy Demos Jones' wife, Phyllis, who alternated weeks singing at Antonio's and the Embers Steak House.

We had a wonderful night with our friends and neighbors, drinking and dancing. We didn't leave Antonio's until ten thirty. When we walked outside, there was an additional four inches of freshly fallen snow on our car. Luckily, the heat was back on in our apartment when we arrived home forty minutes later. The next morning, the snow had stopped, and the local TV station said that the blizzard was a record for the Grand Strand and measured thirteen inches at the airport.

Fast forward eight months. I was in the waiting area of the maternity ward at Ocean View Memorial Hospital in Myrtle Beach. Sitting next to me was Leroy Brunson, whose wife was about to deliver their first son. As fate would have it, Leroy was a cart boy at Possum Trot and a close friend.

Leroy and I became fathers within days of each other. A nurse told me that there were seventeen babies in the ward that week, a ward that had a capacity for eight babies.

Eight months to the day after our dinner at Antonio's, Gracie gave birth to our first son, Gaines Spencer Beard, Jr. Apparently, the record snowstorm of 1973 was a boom for the baby business in Myrtle Beach.

Chapter 8

Q-School

One afternoon in March of 1973, Art emerged from his office and said that he had just gotten off the phone with the director of the Tournament Player's Division of the PGA of America. They were planning a May regional Tour qualifying event, or Q-School in South Carolina. The Dunes Golf and Beach Club, just down the Grand Strand in Myrtle Beach, was chosen as the venue.

Each year, the tournament players' division of the Professional Golfers Association of America conducts a regional qualifier tournament at various courses throughout the country. A dozen or so of the lowest scores from each location proceed to the National Tour Championship, where, after four days of pressure-packed competition, twenty-five young professionals obtain their PGA tour card and the opportunity to compete on the big stage the following year. It is, indeed, a life-altering event with players from across the globe attempting to grab the brass ring.

The Dunes Golf and Beach Club began in 1947 as a dream of local Myrtle Beach businessmen and women who met at a small fishing cabin located on Singleton Swash overlooking the Atlantic Ocean. It is the only golf course in Myrtle Beach with ocean views and was designed by famed architect Robert Trent Jones. From its inception, it has been rated as one of the finest golf courses in the country.

Art said, "Gaines, they are looking for several dozen local PGA members and apprentices to volunteer their services to help run the qualifier."

I said, "If Genny can help you run the shop while I volunteer, then I am in."

Art winked and said, "I'm sure she will be very happy for you to have this experience."

"What would I be doing at the qualifier?"

Art explained that I would be assigned a threesome to follow. I would help determine the procedure if any rule questions were to arise.

A rules official with the PGA of America at Q-School, I was especially excited because, only three months earlier, I had aced the rules examination at the PGA Business School II in West Palm Beach, Florida. The Rules of Golf can get very complicated and tricky with all the possible scenarios that can arise in a round of golf. I was sharp when it came to the penalties and procedures associated with the thirty-four "basic" rules of the game. Knowledge of the rules is a core requirement of being a golf professional.

A few weeks before Q-School, I received a letter from the PGA asking me to give them a call to verify that I still intended to volunteer my services at the qualifier. It went on to list the threesome I would be assigned: an up-and-coming all-American golfer from the University of Alabama, a club professional from a golf course in New Smyrna Beach, Florida, and Peter Oosterhuis, a famous European Tour Professional.

I knew who Peter Oosterhuis was because of the exposure he received a month earlier when he, a British golfer and rookie at Augusta, finished in a tie for third place at The Masters. He was currently the big dog on the European tour, having won the European tour's Order of Merit for the lowest stroke average for the year in 1971 and 1972.

On the morning of the qualifier, I was introduced to my threesome. I was in awe of Peter when we shook hands and exchanged pleasantries. He was a towering figure at six-foot-five inches tall and had an athletic physique. I loved his British accent!

The round went off without the need for my advice until we reached the par three, twelfth hole. At 180 yards, water bordering the right side the entire length, this hole was a test of nerves and skill. Peter lofted a high six-iron toward the right side of the green. It landed six feet onto the front right of the green, sucked back into the fringe, and in what seemed like slow motion, trickled down the bank and into the pond.

When we got to the green, Peter motioned for me to come over and help determine where the ball's drop point should be. We discussed his options and agreed on a spot just off the fringe, no closer to the hole, but still on the slope. He asked me to stand behind him when he dropped the ball and stop it from rolling back into the pond, which I was glad to do. In those days, the legal drop procedure was for the player to stand erect, facing the hole, and blindly drop the ball backward, over his shoulder, without the ball touching the player on the way to the ground.

I stopped the ball from rolling into the water on two consecutive drops and, accordingly, pointed out the spot where the second ball hit the ground. This was the location he must use to place the ball back into play for his next stroke. With a smile, he thanked me and cautiously placed the ball on the spot.

Peter then walked slowly some ten paces up to the hole and, in a sign of confidence, instructed his caddy to remove the pin from the cup.

He studied the slope of the green as he returned to his ball. He took an 8 iron from his bag and, with a putting-like stroke, chipped his ball low onto the green. It landed, took two small bounces, rolled some twenty feet, and came to rest on the very edge of the hole.

As Peter approached the hole to tap the next putt into the cup, a gust of wind caused the ball to waver ever so slightly and enough for the ball to tumble into the cup, untouched. Peter made par on the hole in masterful fashion. At the end of the round, Peter fell short and missed qualifying by two strokes. He went on to continue his dominance of the European tour by winning the Order of Merit twice, again in 1973 and 1974, before earning his tour card in 1975. He was, without a doubt, one of the best players I had ever seen.

Footnote:

In 2012, I took my oldest son, Spencer, to the Ryder Cup matches at the Medinah Country Club in Chicago. The Ryder Cup is a men's golf competition between teams of the best twelve players each from Europe and the United States. The competition is held every two years, with the venue alternating between courses in the United States and Europe.

That year, the Americans held a commanding lead over the Europeans going into Sunday's twelve singles matches. Unfortunately, the U.S. team could not hold off a late charge from the European team and lost the cup on our home soil.

On the flight home to Charlotte, Spencer and I were in first class, seats 1-A and 1-C. We spent the next hour and a half reliving the fabulous week we had together. It was a rare gift, indeed, to have the opportunity to spend quality time with my son since he lived in Mississippi and I in North Carolina.

When we landed in Charlotte and taxied to our gate, I stood up to stretch my legs while waiting on the gangway to be positioned at the door. When I looked around, lo and behold, sitting directly behind me in seat 2-A was none other than Peter Oosterhuis himself. He was returning home to Charlotte after spending the last week as one of the television commentators covering the action at Medinah for NBC. I reintroduced myself, and we chatted about the day he tried to make it through Q-School at the Dunes Club in Myrtle Beach. He said that although he failed to qualify then, he went on to successfully qualify for the America PGA tour the year after that. It's really a small world.

Chapter 9

A Strange Day

The United States Open Championship is a tournament like no other in the world. It is one of the four major golf championships. The thing that sets it apart from every other tournament is the fact that it is open. By open, it means that qualifying is open to any male amateur golfer in the world with a verified handicap of two or less and any golf professional.

Roughly seven thousand golfers attempt to qualify for the championship every year; first, in one of the local qualifiers held throughout the country and on four other continents, narrowing the field down to 550 players. They then compete in a sectional qualifier at several locations throughout the US for 36 holes to determine the final players that will fill out the 156-man roster for the Open.

Many of the players in the field of the US Open are exempt from qualifying due to their past accomplishments or world ranking. That means that thousands of players were competing for only seventy available spots.

I tried to qualify for the US Open six times in the mid to late 70's. In 1973, the local qualifier for North Carolina was at Alamance Country Club in Burlington, just an hour northeast of Salisbury. I played Alamance when I was on the Wingate

College golf team several years earlier. Alamance CC was one of famed architect Donald Ross's true gems. It was a beautiful course with rolling terrain and tight, tree-lined fairways. It has small greens and is a true test of patience and skill.

I was paired with two others that day for the qualifier. Bobby Galloway was a premier player and fellow golf professional in The Carolina's Section of the PGA. Bobby was well known in the Carolinas for his outstanding play and his artistry on the greens. In the late 60's he tried his hand on the PGA Tour as a Monday morning non-exempt player.

A tour non-exempt player is a pro who doesn't have his player's status. He would travel with the tour week-to-week to play in the weekly Monday morning qualifier with hopes of earning one of the few spots available.

In 1965, Bobby qualified for the Memphis Open and went on to finish 10th. In 1972, he won the North Carolina Open, a Carolinas Section of the PGA major championship. I had played several times with Bobby in various CPGA events in the past three years; we were friends.

The other player in our threesome was a standout All-American college golf star from Wake Forest University named Curtis Strange. Curtis was in his third year at Wake Forest and was on a team that Golf World called *The Greatest of all Time,* with teammates Jay Haas and Bob Byman.

Both Curtis and Bobby brought their own caddies. I didn't and had to loop for myself. I had a small Sunday bag and had lightened the load the night before by removing anything that was non-essential: extra balls, knickknacks, and such, but I had to keep my umbrella and rain gear because the weather forecast called for rain in the afternoon.

The sky was overcast on that late May morning. Rain was forecast for the afternoon eighteen holes which meant we had to play well in the morning round to have any chance of snagging one of the six available spots in the hundred-two-man field. If successful, we would advance to the sectionals two weeks later at East Lake Golf Club, at another Donald Ross designated course near downtown Atlanta.

We began the first hole of our thirty-six-hole endurance test with three drives straight down the middle. I remember thinking that those three drives were impressive for a three-some right out of the starting blocks.

I picked up my Sunday bag, put the leather headcover over my beautiful Jack Nicklaus McGregor driver, and headed down the fairway like a man on a mission. A few yards down the fairway, Curtis came up alongside me carrying his bag. I said, "Nice drive, Curtis; I thought you had a caddy."

He grinned, stuck his hand out, and said, "Hey, Gaines, my name is Allan, and I am Curtis' identical twin brother." We started laughing, and I apologized for not paying more attention to what was going on earlier at the tee box. He said, "No worries, it just shows that you were getting yourself focused, which is a good thing." That started what would be an all-day friendship with the Strange brothers.

Both Curtis and I got off to a good start, carding thirty-fives on the front side. Bobby struggled to a forty. One thing I remember about Curtis was his length off the tee. I was a big hitter myself, having won numerous local long-driving contests, but Curtis was LONG. He consistently boomed it twenty-to-thirty yards past me all day. It was not until late in the first round, when we got to a par five hole, that I tried to smash one. I caught that drive in the sweet spot, and at 285 yards, my ball was in a dead heat with Curtis'. That was the only time that day that I tried to catch him. The rest of the day was back to business, hitting fairways and greens.

At the end of eighteen holes, we signed and turned in our scorecards, got a new one and grabbed a quick sandwich on our way over to the first tee to play the final eighteen holes.

Bobby had a bad go of it in the morning round and posted an eight-over-par round of seventy-nine. Curtis fired a one over par seventy-two, and I had a two under par sixty-nine after three-putting the eighteenth hole. I didn't know at the time that I was in sole possession of second place. I would later hear from my wife, Gracie, that she was watching the 5 o'clock news out of Wilmington, NC and heard the sports announcer say, "Local PGA Professional Gaines Beard of North Myrtle Beach fired a scorching 69 in the first round of the United States Open Qualifier in Burlington, NC, one shot back of John Bryant of Charlotte."

By the time we teed off again on number one, the bottom fell out. It was dark and pouring cats and dogs. It was coming down so hard that the five of us gathered under a towering old oak tree alongside the first fairway and waited twenty minutes for it to let up enough for us to continue. We knew it was ok to wait a while without penalty because the group behind us had obviously huddled at the club house and had not yet approached the first tee.

When we got started again, Curtis and I parred the first hole, but Bobby three-putted for a double bogey six. On the second tee box, standing at ten over par with seventeen holes to play, Bobby motioned to his caddy to proceed to the parking lot.

"Fellas, I am finished. I will only be slowing you boys down, and I am too far back to make a run at it. I'm heading to that Cadillac over there."

Shaking hands, he said, "Good luck, Curtis, I enjoyed meeting you. Gaines, a pleasure as always—go get 'em."

With that, he wrote W/D on his card and asked us to turn it in.

It rained off and on the rest of the afternoon. After the end of the round Curtis posted a 72-71=143 and I a 69-75=144. Two-thirds of the field had finished by the time we posted our scores; Curtis was in third place, and I was alone in fourth. It would be another hour and a half before the final threesome would finish. I suggested that we dry off and go into the bar, where I bought us a round of Budweisers in tall, frosted mugs. For the next hour-and-a-half, Curtis, Allan, and I told stories and nibbled on salted peanuts in the exquisite men's lounge with tufted leather chairs and mahogany bar.

They told hilarious tales of their childhood and how, as identical twins, they would occasionally switch classes with one another on test days.

We waited for what seemed an eternity for the final group to finish and post their scores. We chatted about his illustrious amateur career, which included winning the North & South Amateur Championship earlier that year in Pinehurst.

Curtis said, "Gaines, you have a unique name. In fact, I have only known one other Gaines in my life, but it was his last name, Fletcher Gaines."

I said, "I've heard of Fletcher Gaines. Isn't he one of the old caddies at Pinehurst #2?"

"He sure is. He caddied for Tommy Armour, Gene Sarazen and a lot of pros back in the day. Earlier this year, he carried me to victory in the North & South Amateur Championship."

In the end, Curtis moved on to the Sectional Qualifier in Atlanta, and I headed back to North Myrtle Beach, having missed the cut by one stroke.

That would mark the first of three times that I missed qualifying for the Sectionals of the United States Open Championship by a single stroke. The next time was at the Chanticleer Country Club in Greenville, SC, where I shot 72-72-144, and then again at The Pinehurst Country Club courses #1 and #7 with 71-72=143.

Apparently, even par was not good enough to qualify for the U.S. Open. Oddly enough, shooting even par in the U.S. Open Championship on several occasions was good enough to win.

In recent years, the local qualifying changed from 36 holes to just 18. If that were the case when I was competing, I would have advanced to the sectionals twice, if not all three times!

Curtis Strange went on to become one of the greatest players to ever put on a pair of spikes. He won two U.S. Open Championships back-to-back in 1988 and '89. At that time, he became only the second player since World War II to successfully defend the Open title. Before then, only Ben Hogan had accomplished that

Beard misses Open bid by stroke

PINEHURST— Gaines Beard of Salisbury missed by one stroke of qualifying for the U.S. Open golf championship here yesterday. He had rounds of 71 and 72. It marked the third time he has failed to qualify for the Open by one stroke.

Jon Isley and Pete Robison, both of Salisbury, also failed to qualify. Isley had a 152 and Robison turned in a 156.

Gary Hallberg, defending NCCA champion of Wake Forest, led a field of 122 with a 36-hole total of 134 on Pinehurst's No. 1 and 4 courses.

University of North Carolina golfer Kevin King finished one shot behind Hallberg with a 69-66 for a 135. Behind King was David Thore at 136.

Thore also is trying to retain his Professional Golfers' Association card.

In at 139 were Chip Beck and Harvey Ward. Ward is a two-time champion of the National Amateur Open. Cary's Vance Heafner, also trying to earn a PGA card, fired a 140.

Chapter 10

Going To the Big Dance

It was 1974, and since turning pro four years earlier, I had played in numerous professional tournaments conducted by the Carolinas Section of the PGA. Not only was my second-place finish in the sectional Assistants Championship a noted accomplishment, but I also finished second three times in the South Carolina Pro-Pro Championship, a two-man team competition with three different partners.

I finished third low professional in the prestigious Myers Park Country Club Pro-Am held in Charlotte and had a top twenty-five finish in the Carolinas Open, a championship with a field of 350 of the best amateur and professional golfers from the two Carolinas. I had "game" and relished the opportunity to compete.

That fall, Art told me that he and Ginny would leave Possum Trot in the spring to open their own business. Art had the financial backing of several prominent businessmen and planned to open the first Executive Par-3 lighted golf course in the Grand Strand. This enterprise was sure to be successful in this golfing mecca.

The course would have eighteen par three holes scattered throughout rolling hills with lakes and palm trees. None of the holes would be longer than 175 yards- ideal for golfers of all abilities. Lighting would give players the opportunity to enjoy golf under the stars in the crisp coastal night air.

"What am I going to do when y'all leave, Art? Who are they going to get to replace you?"

He replied, "They plan to take over the merchandising and snack bar operations here and hire a general manager to run the day-to-day business. Demus Jones will oversee the operations of both courses, and he will choose my replacement."

Demus, the head pro at our sister club, Robbers Roost, and I were good friends. We were partners in the South Carolina Pro-Pro for one of my three second-place finishes. I figured he would, more than likely, place his assistant pro, Sam Timms, who had been by his side for years, as the general manager at Possum Trot when Art left.

"What do you think I should do?" I repeated.

"I think you should try your hand on the pro circuit," Art said. "You are still young and have plenty of game. Think of how good you could become if all you had to do would be to practice and play golf. There is no telling where your talent might take you. Just look at Leonard."

Leonard Thompson had been an assistant with me under Art in 1971 before he went onto the P.G.A. tour. Before coming to Possum Trot, he had been a standout player for Wake Forest University alongside Joe Inman and Lanny Wadkins, who both became tour stars.

"In less than three years on tour, Leonard won the Jackie Gleason Inverrary Classic just this February," Art pointed out.

"Yeah, but I am no Leonard Thompson. He beat me every time we played together, Art. That is no comparison at all."

Chasing A Dream

"What do you think makes Leonard so much better than you?" Art asked.

"Where do I start? For one, he is bigger and stronger. He drives the ball longer and hits more fairways and greens than I do. There is simply no comparison, period. He has an incredible short game and putts like Nicklaus. I'm not in Leonard's league in any category."

"So, he has better course management than you do. That comes with experience, and I can help you with that. Remember what you told me about your breakfast with Byron Nelson? He said that hitting the fairways and greens was the key to playing your best. You don't have to be big and strong to hit the fairways and greens. You have to use good course management to increase your statistics. As far as your short game and putting are concerned, those just take practice, practice, practice."

"That is all well and good," I said. "But do you really think I could make it through the tour's qualifying tournament and get my player card?"

"Probably not," he said, "but you don't have to get a tour card to try playing on the tour. Your Class "A" PGA card is enough to get you membership into the Tournament Player's Division of the PGA. That means you are eligible to enter the Monday qualifiers for the tournament that begins on Thursday of that week. Typically, eight or more spots open for those in the Monday qualifier competition. If you get into the tournament and make the cut, you don't have to qualify for the following week's event. You are automatically in!"

"No kidding?" I replied. "I think I could do that, not every week, of course, but occasionally, right?"

"Absolutely, but you need to get your game in shape for the pressures of competition. Here's what I would do if I were you…" Art offered. "In late November, I would go to Florida and play on the Florida Winter Tour. You would travel across northern Florida, playing in an event every week or two. The good news: less than a hundred guys play that tour. There is no Monday morning qualifying. Just pay the entry fee and tee it up. You could do that for a couple of months until the big tour moves from California to Florida in February."

"That sounds good, but I have a family to think about now. I don't have the money to fund my tour efforts and support my family simultaneously." I sighed.

"Don't you think your parents could help you out?" he asked. "There is also the possibility that some of the Salisbury Country Club members back home could band together and sponsor you on the tour."

"Exactly how does that work, Art?"

"It takes approximately twenty thousand dollars annually to pay for tour expenses and family responsibilities. You need to get ten people to invest two thousand dollars each to own ten percent of your tour effort. Tournament earnings go directly to the sponsors' bank account until you return their investment. Thereafter, your sponsors receive fifty percent of the profits."

"I get it. No one individual is on the hook for a lot of money, and I am sure to make some money, at least on the Florida Winter Tour."

Once again, I was facing a life-changing career decision, but this time I wasn't alone. I had a wife and newborn son to think about. What would Gracie think about me leaving them to galivant around Florida, trying to make a living playing golf?

Chasing A Dream

Surely, she would rather I find another pro job in Myrtle Beach without turning the life we were now enjoying upside down. I could find another job, but the thought of playing professional golf was too hard to ignore. If not now, I reasoned, then when?

That night, I told Gracie about my conversation with Art and asked what she thought.

"If you get the sponsors, then I think we should go for it. We can move to Columbia and live with my parents while we see how it goes. I could even get a part-time job with mother there to help with Spencer."

Hurdle number one went smoother than I had imagined. I now needed a plan to get sponsors. I decided to go home to Salisbury on Monday and talk with an attorney about writing up a sponsorship contract.

I was excited by the possibility of playing on the PGA tour. I couldn't wait to give my mother the good news. Arriving home just after five p.m., at happy hour, I was sure to find my mother sitting up front in the library, smoking a Salem, waiting for Seth to get home and fix cocktails.

When I entered the library, my mother sat in her favorite wing-back chair, with one leg tucked under her and a Salem cigarette dangling from her red-painted lips. She was working to create a new crossword puzzle for the New York Times Sunday magazine. My mother's hobby was crossword puzzle construction. Her puzzles had previously been published in the Sunday Times magazine four times, an incredible feat for someone who did not attend college. She barely noticed my presence.

"Darling boy, there you are. Come give me a kiss," she said, laying the cigarette and puzzle aside and reaching for my face. After I kissed her cheek, she said, "It will be your pleasure to make your mother a drink and meet me on the front porch."

I went to the pantry, made us both a bourbon and water and met her out front. Mom loved sitting on the glider sofa with her cocktail and cigarette while holding court with her friends and family in the evenings. Since it was just the two of us, it was a good time to tell Mom about my desire to play professional golf and my plan to get sponsorship funds.

"You are NOT going to ask my friends to give you money!" Mom said indignantly. "I will not have that embarrassment."

My mother, Mary Marshall, was a Grande Dame in Salisbury, president of the Historic Salisbury Foundation, member of the Mayflower Society, and past president of the North Carolina chapter of the Daughters of the American Revolution. She was not about to have her son telling her friends that he needed money.

"But Mom, it isn't asking for money; it's asking for sponsorship for expenses on tour for a year. Each sponsor would own a share in the endeavor. It's like owning part of a racehorse," I explained.

"Still, I don't want any of my friends to gamble their money on my son. So, here's what I will do. Do you still have Aunt Nena DeBerry's twelve place settings of sterling silver?"

"Of course," I replied, knowing where this was going.

"Give me the silver, and I will give you the money I have in savings, eight thousand dollars. That should be enough money for you to test the waters."

I thought for a moment about looking for sponsors, no matter what my mother thought. After all, these people were my friends, too.

I found myself with a decision that had no options. I had to take my mother's deal if I wanted to maintain a good relationship with her. It was better than nothing, considering I had no idea how the sponsorship efforts would have worked out.

I returned to North Myrtle with plans to better my chances of success come November. Art kept his word, allowing me ample opportunities to practice and work on my game. He would often stay after work to watch me hit range balls until dark, and then we'd go to the Embers for a drink to discuss my progress and future practice schedule. Art was a great teacher and pushed me hard to work on my short game and putting.

"Gaines," he said, "putting is the most important part of the game. There are eighteen holes on a golf course. If you were to play a "regulation" round of golf, hit every green in regulation, two putts every green, you would shoot an even-par score. That means you are using a putter for thirty-six strokes of the round. Par for eighteen holes is seventy-two; therefore, half of the strokes are made with the putter. The better you can putt, the better you will score."

I worked on my game as often as I could those last few months of 1974. A week before I was to head south to Florida, Art said that he and Ginny wanted to take me and Gracie out for a farewell dinner. He said for us to meet them at The Old Pro's Table, a favorite haunt of the golfing crowd, the next evening at seven.

The thought of leaving Art and Ginny again gave me sadness. I wanted to make a respectable showing in my new quest, not only for me and my family but for Art as well. He put a lot of time into my training and had faith in me. He was the perfect mentor.

Gracie and I arrived at The Old Pro's Table just before seven. When we reached the door, I saw a sign that read "Private Party," but I didn't give it a second thought. I opened the door for Gracie and saw a banner that read,

"Good Luck, Gaines and Gracie." Holding it, at one end were Art and Ginny, and at the other end were Seth and my mother! Behind them were forty friends and relatives yelling, "SURPRISE!"

A surprise it was. Never in my wildest dreams could I imagine a surprise going away party for us. With my parents were my little sister Katherine, brother Bryce, his wife Patti, and my great-aunt Julia from Columbia. In the crowd were the owners of Possum Trot and Robbers Roost, several golf pros with their wives, a few club members, and local friends. Vernon & Phillis, who usually performed at the Embers Steak House, were there to support us with their music and songs.

Toward the end of the dinner, Phillis passed the microphone around to those who wanted to wish us well or tell a story involving me or Gracie. It was an incredible ego boost to have so many people show their love and support. The last person to give a toast was Art. He gave an emotional speech about how much I meant to them and how much we would be missed. He applauded my hard work and dedication. I had to fight back tears, hearing such wonderful things being said about me. At the end of his speech, Art surprised us once again.

"Let's show our support with more than words. Send this young couple off with a little extra money in their war chest. See that glass jar at the front desk? Fill it with your love and support."

The twelve hundred dollars we received that night gave us almost ten thousand dollars to start the next chapter in our lives. A week later, I would be off to play in the Cypress Gardens Open in Winter Haven, Florida.

Gaines Beard

Chapter 11

But The Band Didn't Play

The drive to Winter Haven, Florida, home of the state's oldest tourist attraction, Cypress Gardens, took ten hours. Located just southwest of Orlando, it was famous for its botanical gardens and world-renowned waterskiing exhibitions.

I arrived at dusk on a Wednesday evening, checked into a Motel 6 on the interstate, grabbed a bite to eat at Hardee's, and turned in for the evening. I had a ten o'clock tee time the next morning in the one-day pro-am. Having not played the course before, I was using the pro-am round as my practice round before the three-day tournament.

Arriving ninety minutes before my tee time gave me ample time to loosen up my muscles, tight from the long trip. I hit about a hundred balls and practiced my putting and chipping before heading over to the starter's table to meet my three amateur partners.

One of the guys made a big impression on me. Sylvester was a black gentleman in his early thirties. He stood six-foot-three and had an athletic build. He had with him his "posse." Three of his golfing friends were tagging along to cheer him on.

"Hey, pro," one of them said, "Have you got game? 'Cause Sylvester here has played in this pro-am four years now, and he beat all four of the pros before you."

"That's awesome," I replied, "Hope Sylvester plays great again today, and if I hang with him, we'll cash a check. That's what I'm talking about," as I high-fived the guys.

It was perfect weather for golf, and I was with a great group of fellas. I had dreamed of playing well in my first event, thus validating my ability to compete on the big stage. When the round was over, the posse was, once again, proud of their man.

Sylvester shot a two under par seventy. The other two players in our group did not contribute much to our best ball score. I, however, had the competitive round of my young career, a six under sixty-six, which earned second in the individual pro division, one shot back of Gary Groh. He had been a star player for Michigan State University.

He went on to win the Hawaiian Open three months later and played in both the U.S. Open and the Masters, two of the four major championships in professional golf.

Our pro-am team posted a ten under par score, which was good enough for a tie for seventh place. My second-place finish in the pro division paid sixty dollars and our team finish netted us forty dollars each. We had a couple of beers in the bar after the round.

"Sylvester," I said, "your boys put the pressure on me from the get-go. That must be the reason I played so well."

"Hell, pro, you're a bad man. You got game." Sylvester said with his beer held high. We had a great day together. Sylvester said he would come out and watch me play on Saturday, his day off.

One hundred dollars may not sound like a lot of money but considering that my motel room was six-ninety-five a night and gasoline only thirty cents a gallon, it was, indeed, a profitable day. Returning to my room with a six-pack of Miller beer, I immediately placed a collect call to Art to tell him about my day.

"Are you going to call me collect every time you play well?" Art asked.

"I hope I call you every day. That means I'm making money and can pay you for the calls." I said laughingly. "Keep a running tab, and I will pay you back."

"No, you won't," he said. "I'll enjoy the ride with you, so please keep me posted. Congratulations, son."

After three days of tournament play, my top twenty-five finish paid seventy-five dollars. The next tournament would start in four days at New Smyrna Golf Club in New Smyrna Beach, just south of Daytona. I spent the next day practicing in Winter Haven and getting some needed rest.

I didn't fare well at New Smyrna and was not in the money. The next tournament would be in two weeks, so I went back to Columbia to spend time with my family.

Vergil Smith, the pro at Spring Valley Country Club in Columbia, was a former assistant pro at the Surf Golf and Beach Club in North Myrtle Beach. We had been friends for years. Vergil knew that we had moved to Columbia while I was trying my hand at playing the tour. Needing a place to practice while back home, I reached out to Vergil. He said there would be no problem for me to play and practice at Spring Valley if he could tell the board of directors that I was a part-time assistant pro.

"That way, Gaines, you would have access to the entire club as my employee. You would not be on my payroll, but they don't have to know that. I'd ask you to watch the shop while I give lessons or on my lunch break, things like that. How does that sound?"

"Great, Verg, I'll help you out any way I can. Thanks a lot, pal!"

Having access to a great country club for practice while in town was exactly what I needed. I took full advantage of my good fortune and went to the club every day at eight in the morning.

I was helping Vergil so much that he started keeping track of my hours. As I was about to head back to Florida, Vergil handed me a check for two hundred dollars and said that our arrangement would stand as long as I wanted.

I spent the next several months traveling back and forth between Columbia and Florida in my '63 Chevy, eating hot dogs and occasionally sleeping in my car. I made several good friends in Florida, and we would often share a motel room to save money.

Beau Baugh was my first roomie. He was the younger brother of the LPGA tour's star Laura Baugh, who was the "It Girl" on the women's tour because of her beauty and golfing ability. Before joining the LPGA tour, she had won the United States Women's Amateur Championship at the age of sixteen, the youngest to do so in the 76-year history of the event. A year before I met Beau, Laura was the tour's Rookie of the Year.

Another fella I roomed with was Nathanial "Nate" Starks. He was one of the few black golfers playing professionally. We called him "Sarge" because he had served in the US Army. I took an instant liking to Nate, and the feeling was mutual.

We became fast friends and would hang out in the evenings with several of the other black professionals playing the winter tour, among them Bobby Stroble and George Johnson. George had his tour card and was playing the winter tour while waiting for the big tour's east coast swing. Many a night, we would play cards with the guys in our room 'til after midnight. They accepted me without prejudice as I did them. We had a lot of laughs together and rooted for one another to play well.

I earned just under two thousand dollars during my three months traveling around northern Florida. It wasn't enough to cover my expenses, and my war chest was down to seventy-five hundred dollars. I was going to have to play better and spend less if I wanted to continue pursuing my dream.

In late February, the PGA Tour moved from the west coast to begin its east coast swing. On February 27th, I would be attempting to qualify for the Jackie Gleason Inverrary Classic in Lauderhill, Florida. This was the site of Leonard Thompson's first tour win just a year earlier.

My traveling expenses were sure to increase, and the distance from Columbia to southern Florida meant fewer trips home to see my family. Starting with the Gleason, the next three events were the Florida Citrus Open in Orlando, the Doral Eastern Airlines Open in Miami, and the Greater Jacksonville Open.

I failed to qualify for those four events. After missing out in Jacksonville, I headed back home to Columbia to see my family and get some needed rest. Fortunately, the next tournament that I planned to enter would be the Greater Greensboro Open in Greensboro, North Carolina.

My trips to Florida were over for now, and with little to show for my efforts, my spirits were low. I started to doubt whether I was cut out to be a professional golfer. Sure, I had some very good success in the Carolinas, but this was the "Big Stage." Gracie did her best to pump me up. She saw my disappointment and shared my concerns.

"Look, honey, it's not the end of the world. You have six more tournaments scheduled before the Kemper in Charlotte on June 5th. We have enough money to get us through June, but if you are not successful, then we always have plan "B." Plan B was to give up trying to play pro golf, get a club job, and settle down.

"The week after Greensboro is the Magnolia Classic in Hattiesburg, Mississippi. That's when Spencer and I will start traveling with you!" Gracie said with excitement.

Gracie's big sister, Betty Jo Cotten, and her family lived in Hattiesburg. We were going to stay with them for a week. Betty Jo's oldest son, Miles, wanted to caddy for me, so our expenses for that week would be next to nothing. The tournament was at the Country Club of Hattiesburg, where the Cottens were members. At sixteen years old, Miles had played a lot of golf there and knew the course well.

On Sunday, the day before qualifying, Miles and I went to the club to play a practice round. I could sense he was nervous to be caddying in a professional tournament.

"OK, pal, here's the deal. All you have to do is carry the bag and rake the traps just like you do every day when you play. I may ask you a question every now and then, like, what's beyond that hill, or does this putt break to the right, stuff like that. Easy, right?"

"Sure thing, pro. I can do that. I'll try not to talk unless you ask me something," Miles said confidently.

"We're going to have a good time together, Miles," I replied.

We played the practice round, and Miles did great. The course was in excellent shape, and I felt comfortable on it. On Monday, I fired an even par round of 72 and qualified for my first pro tour event! We were all excited as this had now turned into a family affair.

On Thursday, I got off to a rough start and shot 76. I would have to go low on Friday if I were to have any chance of making it to the weekend. The forecast for Friday called for rain. That didn't bode well for my chances of shooting a low round.

As predicted, rain came, and along with it, thunder and lightning. The siren blew, indicating we must leave the golf course and seek shelter. Luckily, we were on the ninth green at the time and could shelter in the clubhouse instead of someone's back porch somewhere along the course.

Inside, about fifty of us players gathered in the club's main dining room to wait out the storm. I was at a table with four other guys where the topic of conversation centered around the impact Arnold Palmer had on the increased purses and television coverage of the current tour.

"Arnie's popularity with the fans has no doubt affected the amount of prize money we play for these days," Fuzzy Zoeller said. "If it weren't for Arnie, we would still be playing for peanuts."

Alan Tapie, sitting next to me, said, "Bull, you can't give Arnie the credit for that. TV coverage has increased, and people love Jack Nicklaus, Tony Lima, Chi Chi, and a lot of other players, too."

"Look here, Wormy," (that's what we called Tapie) "if Arnold Palmer was playing here in Hattiesburg-by-God Mississippi, half the businesses in town would have a *Closed for the Afternoon* sign in the window, and they would be out here following him." Chuckling, I continued. "Look behind you. That's Orville Moody, a United States Open Champion, and you could drive his gallery in here on a motorcycle. Don't tell me Arnie hasn't had a big impact on the money we play for today."

After a two-hour delay, I completed my round with a 75 and missed the cut for the low seventy players and ties. I was dejected and down on myself once again. I had missed an opportunity to make the cut and earn some prize money. More importantly, however, I would have also been exempt from qualifying the next week in Tallahassee.

On Saturday, I drove Gracie and Spencer back home. Sunday morning, I headed out, once again, to Florida for the Tallahassee Open.

I qualified for the tournament, shooting a 72. On Thursday, I played my heart out, shooting a 70, placing me tied for fifteenth after round one.

That night was only the third time that I called Art with good news after a round. The second time was a week earlier when I qualified at Hattiesburg.

Sleep didn't come easily that night. Thinking about letting my family down the week earlier, I tossed and turned. On Friday, I shot a miserable 76 and missed the cut once again, this time by a single stroke.

I headed back home with my tail between my legs. To Gracie's credit, she never once expressed disappointment in my failures. She was always upbeat and positive, saying things like, "Don't worry, honey. Your time will come." The First NBC New Orleans Open was one of the biggest events on tour and naturally had great television coverage. Gracie, Spencer, and I drove there on Saturday, giving me an opportunity to play a practice round on Sunday. We checked into a very nice motel near the course. I wanted Gracie to, at least, be comfortable if we were to be here for, hopefully, a week.

That week's Monday qualifier had a total of one hundred and twelve pros playing for just seven spots in the tournament. On Sunday, before my practice round, a nice young man named Jerry approached me in the parking lot and asked if I had a caddy. I told him that I didn't, so we teamed up for this tournament. We agreed on forty-five dollars a day for his services.

As fate would have it, I was given a one-twenty tee time for the qualifier. I knew that when we made the turn, after nine holes at the clubhouse, two-thirds of the field would have finished with their scores posted on the scoreboard. We would have a good idea of how I stood with nine holes to play.

We got off to a great start with bookend birdies. After birdies on the first and ninth holes, with seven pars in between, I was two under par with nine to play. As we passed the scoreboard on our way to the tenth tee, I noticed that the lowest score so far was 68, and the seventh lowest score was one over par 73. If we could finish under par, I was sure to make my third tournament start in a row.

On the back nine, I remained two under par going into the seventeenth hole, a two-hundred-yard par three. I pulled my three-iron left and landed in a greenside bunker. After blasting out and missing my six-foot par putt, I was one under par with one hole to play.

Standing on the eighteenth tee, I realized I needed no worse than bogey to qualify. I hit my best drive of the day, long and in the dead center of the fairway. We had one-hundred-forty-five yards to the middle of the green. I pulled an eight-iron out of the bag and waited for my two playing companions to hit their shots. Out of the blue, Jerry said,

"Pro, I think you have too much club in your hand. You should hit a nine iron because your adrenaline is flowing, and you are pumped up. You'll knock that eight-iron over the green."

I putt the eight iron back into the bag and took out the nine. My shot landed short of the green in a bunker. After blasting out of the sand and then three-putting, I walked off the eighteenth green with a double-bogey six and a round of 73, one over par. I missed qualifying by one stroke and was boiling inside. If Jerry had done what caddies are supposed to do; Don't offer advice unless you are asked, I surely would not have made worse than bogey and qualified.

Jerry had tears in his eyes as I handed him the forty-five dollars. He was apologizing as hard as he could and even tried to give me back my money.

"Jerry," I said, "it could have happened to anybody. You thought you were right, and you certainly didn't do it on purpose. I am the one who agreed with your reasoning and hit the shot; don't beat yourself up over it." We shook hands, but what I truly wanted to do was strangle him. I did a great job hiding my anger. When I arrived back at the motel, I sat there for a moment; still in shock, I banged the steering wheel with my hands and yelled at the top of my lungs words that rarely crossed my lips. When I entered the room and saw Gracie and Spencer sitting there in anticipation, I erupted into tears and fell into the bed, sobbing like a baby. I had never been more disappointed in my life. I was a complete failure and a broken man. That was the first time that suicide crossed my mind, but I knew I had too much to live for.

In the next three weeks, I failed to qualify in Memphis, Atlanta, and Charlotte. I returned home to Columbia to, once again, change the course of my life.

Chapter 12

Moving On

Back in Columbia, with my dreams of playing professional golf in the rear-view mirror, I went to work full-time at Spring Valley while searching for a head professional position in the Carolinas.

Gracie was glad to finally have me home. She could sense my disappointment in not achieving my dream of playing golf for a living. Her parents were also very understanding and supportive and let me have whatever time I needed to heal and move on. We were welcome in their home for as long as we wanted

Not long after returning to Columbia, I was helping Gracie's dad, Jim, with the yard work. I had just finished mowing the back yard when he approached me with a couple of glasses of lemonade in his hand.

"Gaines, I want to talk with you; let's take a break." He walked me over to a white wrought iron bench that encircled an old oak tree in the center of the yard. "I know that you're disappointed, but you have nothing to be ashamed of. You play golf at a level that most people could never achieve. You can hold your head high, Gaines. You gave it a shot, knowing all along that the odds were stacked against you, but you tried anyway."

As I hung my head, nodding in agreement, he said, "If you hadn't tried, you would have regretted not giving it a chance for the rest of your life, I promise you. The what-ifs in life don't do anyone any good. You know what they say, it's better to have tried and failed than to never have tried at all...something like that." He stood up, patted me on the shoulder, and went back inside.

I interviewed for several head pro positions that summer. One was in Lake Lure, North Carolina. That job went to an older former tour player. Another interview was in Fripp Island, South Carolina. It went to Hamp Auld, a seasoned professional from South Carolina.

Three months after returning, I was offered the head professional and general manager's position at New Ellenton Country Club near Aiken, South Carolina. New Ellenton is a small community that came about when the U.S. government forced 6000 residents to relocate and move their homes and buildings away from the construction site of the Savannah River Project (SRP) in the early 1950s. Until the end of the Cold War, the SRP was a Department of Energy facility focused on the production of plutonium and tritium for use in the manufacture of nuclear weapons.

New Ellenton Country Club was a nine-hole golf course with a log cabin barracks-style clubhouse. The club only had thirty to forty members and depended on greens fee play to survive. My charge was to breathe new life into the club that was suffering financially.

Gracie and I rented a nice ranch-style home in a quiet neighborhood not far from the club. It was fully furnished and sat on three-quarters of an acre with tall, majestic pine trees in the yard. We were comfortable in New Ellenton and became good friends with the owners of the club, J.B. and Betty Standridge. They loved Spencer and insisted on babysitting him whenever Gracie was helping me in the shop or when we would go to Aiken or Augusta for dinner and a movie. New Ellenton was a "country" golf club, not a country club in the true sense of the term. It did not have tennis courts or a pool, nor did it have a driving range, kitchen, or snack bar. The only employee was me. The owners, JB and his co-owner Ray, would mow the fairways and keep the tractors and equipment in repair. A high-school boy named Mark would mow the greens a couple of evenings during the week and on weekends. Albert, a retiree of SRP, had helped JB and Ray run the shop before I came on board. I kept him on part-time, so I could play with the members and go to an occasional golf tournament.

A week before coming to New Ellenton, I nearly won the South Carolina Open. My high finish made the local community proud of their new golf pro.

SWINGING PRO
Gaines Beard has taken over the pro duties at the New Ellenton Country Club. (Staff Photo By Scott Hunter)

Former Pro Tour Player Is Now New Ellenton Pro

By SCOTT HUNTER
Sports Editor

From fudgecicles to hot dogs, from an assistant club pro's job to the pro tour; Gaines Beard has tried them all.

Beard is the new golf pro at the New Ellenton Country Club. The 26-year-old native of Salisbury, N.C., has been at the course since Sept. 1.

The pro said recently that he has been involved in golf for about 15 years now. It was fudgecicles and other goodies, he said, offered as a bribe by his brother, that got him hooked on the game.

"It's my life now," he said. "I really enjoy golf."

Beard, after attending Wingate College in Char- served the years of apprenticeship needed to get a Class A certificate. He took the New Ellenton job, he said, because it is a challenge.

"There was no one here before me to be compared with," he explained. "It's a chance to do what I think is needed to improve the place. I really enjoy it. The people here are just super."

Beard said he hopes to organize the club so that more activities are available to the members.

"In the past, we haven't had any promotion," he explained. "The owners all work and don't have the free time like I do. I want to organize the club into a work- bership and to possibly add an additional nine holes.

The regular initiation fee of $75, Beard said, will be waived for a 60-day period. Singles can now join the club for $150 per year, while families can join for $180 per year.

Should the membership increase as planned, the pro said another nine holes could be added within the next three years.

"We have the land for nine more holes and we have an architect," he said.

About New Ellenton's current layout, he remarked, "From what I hear, it's one of the better nine-hole courses in the area.

"It's not flat," he continu-

Beard Trails By 1

Horne's 68 Nabs State Open Lead

By HAROLD MARTIN
State Sports Writer

BEAUFORT — Veteran amateur Dick Horne of Mt. Pleasant slashed out a four-under-par 68 Thursday over the sporty Pleasant Point Plantation course and vaulted into the lead after two rounds in the annual South Carolina Open golf tournament.

Horne, often a top challenger in major area events but still searching for his first big triumph, racked up a 36-hole total of 140, four under par, to earn a one-stroke advantage over Gaines Beard of New Ellenton two-thirds of the way through the 54-hole event that winds up today.

Beard, who has just been testing himself on the tour in recent months but has just accepted a club job at New Ellenton Country Club, had rounds of 70-71 and appeared to have edged in front until Horne, playing in the day's final foursome, posted his 68 to nab first place.

2-B Columbia, S.C.,
Friday, August 22, 1975

Courtesy of The State

    I used every trick in the book to bolster the membership of the club. We had membership drives at discount rates, hosted golf tournaments, and held their first-ever member-guest tournament, complete with a catered dinner and a live team auction for prize monies, known as a Calcutta.

    We created a snack bar with the usual crackers, peanuts, beer, and soft drinks, etc. Gracie made ham and cheese and pimento cheese sandwiches. I put in a hotdog machine and provided slaw, relish, and chopped onions along with the regular condiments.

    Despite our efforts to grow the club, getting people to join a nine-hole golf course in less than pristine condition was a hard sell. After a year in New Ellenton, the owners and I mutually agreed to part ways. Gracie, Spencer, and I moved back to my hometown of Salisbury to live with my mother and stepfather until I got my ducks in a row.

    Salisbury was my home, and I loved it there. Gracie and I made friends easily and had a good social circle. We were in a bridge club and a canasta club and joined the Country Club of Salisbury just weeks after arriving in town.

Instead of going to work for my family in the conveyor and bottling equipment business, I borrowed enough money from my grandfather's trust to open the Gaines Beard's Discount Golf Center and Club Repair on West Innes Street, just three doors down from the town square.

I was an excellent refinisher of wooden clubheads and had a good repair business. Sales of new clubs and equipment were not so profitable. I had difficulty stocking my shop with top-of-the-line equipment because, in those days, only golf course pro shops could sell the top name brands.

My refinished Jack Nicklaus 271 persimmon driver

In the spring of 1977, I was playing the best golf of my life. In a few weeks, the Greater Greensboro Open was to be played at the Forest Oaks Country Club. I still had the itch to try my hand at qualifying for a big tour event, especially one in my own backyard. I was planning to apply for my amateur status soon, so this might be my last opportunity to try my hand at pro golf.

The qualifying golf course would be The Cardinal in Greensboro. It is one of the most challenging golf courses in the state. I had played it once before and walked off scratching my head at what a great course it was. Qualifying scores would surely be higher than at most venues.

The GGO was the first week of April, one week before The Masters tournament in Augusta, Georgia. The field would be the best in the world, full of players honing their game the week before the year's first major.

I began practicing every chance I got. I had recently bought a Zebra mallet head putter. I was rolling the ball great and making my share of putts, and my ball striking was the best it had ever been. I could hit it high or low and fade or draw it on command. With my good putting, I believed I had the best chance ever to qualify and make the cut. If ever I was ready, it was now.

The Sunday before the Monday qualifier, I went to play a practice round at The Cardinal. Jake, a junior member of the club, offered to caddy for me for two days. He was a senior in high school and on the golf team. I liked Jake a lot and saw a little bit of me in him. We had a good practice round, and I felt ready for the challenge.

That night at dinner, I told Gracie that I felt great about my chances the next day.

"That's the spirit, honey," she said. "This isn't like all the other times when you were trying so hard to make a living at it. This time, you have a job and are now doing it for the fun and challenge of it."

"I know, Gracie, but wouldn't it be awesome if I made it happen right here in Greensboro? Our friends and family could come out and watch me play. What an experience that would be!"

"Yes but try not to think about that. Just go out there and concentrate on your game and have fun."

I arrived at the course the next morning an hour and a half before my tee time. To my surprise, Jake was already there and eager to caddy in a "pro event." We went to the putting green and practiced putting and chipping for thirty minutes. Then we went to the range, and I went through the bag, hitting every club at least four times: high, low, left, and right. We went back to the putting green fifteen minutes before tee-off. I was ready.

At a par of 71, The Cardinal was all the golf course you would want. It's located on wooded undulating land with a stream meandering through it. With two lakes and severe bunkering, the slightest errant shots could end up costing you.

I would be playing the back nine first in the double tee format. Jake and I got off to a fast start, birdieing three holes on the back side, making the turn posting a two-under-par 34. On the front nine, after six pars and one bogey, I reached the difficult par three eighth, my seventeenth hole, one under par with two holes left to play.

Number eight was 195 yards long. The green was elevated and surrounded by tall oak trees. A stream ran in front of the green, and there were bunkers short and to the left.

I stood there, planning my tee shot, when my mind suddenly leap-frogged to "Here we go again." I had been in this situation several times before. The most recent at the New Orleans Open, and I knew how that had turned out. Taking a deep breath, I said to myself, "Not this time!"

"Give me the three-iron, Jake. I'm going to hit it in the middle of the green. Put a good swing on it," he said. I addressed the ball and went through my normal pre-shot routine: TARGET...STANCE...HEAD...BALANCE...SWING.

I didn't hit it as solidly as I needed to. In shock and disbelief, I watched the ball land just short of the green and slowly trickle back into the stream. In an instant, a million thoughts raced through my mind, none of them positive. I shook my head like a dog flapping its ears to gather myself and repeated the words, "Not this time!"

As Jake and I walked toward the creek, I was gathering all the positive thoughts that I could muster. "Be positive," I told myself. "You can get this up-and-down for a bogey and be even par for the round with one hole to play."

After taking my penalty drop, I hit a good chip shot that ended up five feet above the hole. The putt was a slick downhiller breaking slightly to the left. I hit what I thought was a good putt, but the ball lipped the cup, and I made a double bogey!

Instead of being totally crushed, I looked Jake square in the eyes and said, "OK, let's go birdie the last hole!"

After a perfect drive and solid four iron, I was left with a twelve-foot birdie putt for an even par round of 71. After reading the break from every angle imaginable, a calm feeling set in. It was one of those indescribable feelings that a golfer rarely gets, but when it happens, you just know you are going to make the putt. You can just "feel" it.

Dead Center. I finished with a birdie and an even par round of 71.

Chapter 13

The Playoff

When Jake and I left the eighteenth green to turn in our scorecard, we were the third to the last group of the day on the golf course. We would not have to wait long to see if I had qualified.

Upon entering the scorer's tent, I saw the leaderboard. There were two scores under par: a 69 and a 70. At even par 71, there were already six posted, and mine made the seventh.

After waiting a half hour, all scores were in. In a field of 112 golfers playing for only seven spots, 69 and 70 were automatically in. That left seven players vying for five spots in a sudden-death playoff. We were told to be on the first tee in twenty minutes.

I took a close look at the board to see who I would be playing against in the playoff. After all, with seven men playing for five spots the odds were very good. I only had to beat two guys to be able to play in the Greater Greensboro Open, just miles from my hometown.

On the list was Jack Lewis, Jr., one of the most talented golfers to ever play golf at Wake Forest University. His list of accomplishments in junior golf in the Carolinas was astonishing. He only lost one individual match in his entire college career. He had played in the Masters in 1967 and 1968 as an Amateur!

Other prominent names that shot 70 that day were Lon Hinkle, Marty Fleckman and, lo and behold, my old pal from the Florida mini-tour days, Nathaniel "Nate" Starks.

We left the scorer's tent and headed to the putting green for a little practice. There was Nate, and upon recognizing me, he dropped his putter and came toward me with arms open. We hugged and said our hellos. I asked, "Nate, how the hell you been, man?"

"Gaines, I've been well, but my golf game hasn't been great lately."

"I see you shot 71 today and are in the playoff. Man, that's great!" I said.

"How did you do?" he asked.

"I doubled number eight but birdied nine to shoot 71, also." I grinned.

"Awesome, dude, just like the old days, right? The last time we saw each other was a couple of years ago in Tallahassee. I recall we both shot 70 in the first round of that tournament."

"Yep," I replied. "We had a couple beers after the round to celebrate. You went on to make the cut, and I missed it by a stroke, as I remember."

"That's right. I wondered where you've been, not seeing you around and all."

```
TALLAHASSSEE, Fla. (AP) — Here
are the results Thursday after the fist
round of the $60,000 Tallahassee Open,
being played on the 7,124-yard par-72 Kill-
earn Golf and Country Club course. (A—
denotes amateur.):
Steve Melnyk             34-33—67
Ralph Johnston           33-34—67
John Toepel              34-33—67
Bob Shaw                 33-34—67
Bobby Mitchell           34-33—67
Rik Massengale           32-35—67
Larry Wise               35-33—68
Alan Taple               34-34—68
Jim Marshal"             34-34—68
Spike Kelley             34-35—69
Sammy Rachels            35-34—69
Larry Nelson             33-36—69
Mike Long                35-34—69
Bert Yancey              34-35—69
Terry Dill               35-35—70
Ross Randall             35-35—70
Nate Starkes             37-33—70
Bobby Walzel             36-34—70
Ed Dougherty             33-37—70
Wally Armstrong          35-35—70
Bruce Baird              36-34—70
Gaines Beard             36-34—70
Bunky Henry              34-36—70
David Graham             36-35—71
Terry Small              35-36—71
Mason Rudolph            34-37—71
Fred Marti               37-34—71
Mike Morley              36-34—71
Austin Straub            37-34—71
John Aberdroth           35-36—71
Joe Porter               37-34—71
Florentino Molina        38-33—71
Rich Bland               37-34—71
Frank Connor             36-35—71
Bob Charles              36-35—71
Pete Brown               35-36—71
Jim Whittenberg          36-35—71
Dan Sikes                37-34—71
Jay Horton               34-37—71
Jim Dent                 36-35—71
Bruce Fleisher           35-36—71
```

I told him about New Ellenton, my golf center, and how I was at peace with myself after leaving the tour caravan.

"It's a tough road out here; I don't have to tell you that. After earning my tour card at the tour qualifying school last year, I got a sponsor who put up $25,000 to fund me. It's a strange thing, Gaines. I thought that having a sponsor would take some of the pressure off, but for me, it's the opposite. Now, when I play, I'm not just playing for me and my family, but for him, too. It's a bitch, man."

"How have you been doing since getting him?"

"I've made about seven grand, but if I don't get it in gear, Mr. Horne will be in the wind tending to his drug stores in Florida, and I will be left high and dry. I can't do it on my own."

The seven of us gathered on the first tee for the playoff as an official explained the rules. We drew numbers from a hat to see who would hit first, second and so on. Nate was in the first foursome, and I was in a threesome following them.

Number one at The Cardinal is a 420-yard par four. The hole slopes down into a valley and then rises steeply up to the green. The three of us watched as the foursome in front of us played their tee shots and second shots to the green. From our elevated location, we could see where the players hit their shots. It was evident that two of the four would have to scramble to make pars. I felt sure that if I parred the hole, I would be in.

Just as I had done earlier, I hit a perfect drive down the left side some 310 yards onto the fairway. When Jake and I reached my drive, I commented, "Jake, I'll be damned. There's my divot from when we played earlier, right?"

"Sure is," he said laughingly. "You could throw a blanket over your two drives on this hole."

"OK, we have 110 yards to the hole, just like last time. I hit a sand wedge pin high."

"That's right, but the air is heavier now late in the day. I think you should hit the pitching wedge to be safe."

My mind flashed back to New Orleans when my caddy suggested the nine iron instead of the eight that I wanted to hit. I listened to him and made a double bogey.

"You are right, but I'm jacked up, and I think this is enough club." I hit it solidly, but this time, my caddy was right. The ball landed on top of the slope and ended up at the bottom of the hill. I had a blind thirty-yard chip shot that I hit ten feet from the hole. "Hole it, and I'm in, I thought." My putt lipped the cup, and I made bogey.

I was tired of always coming close, and I was pissed. I tried to conceal my anger, but how much could I take? What did I do to deserve all the near misses I've had in my golfing career? I knew there wasn't any answer.

In a fleeting instant, all my past failures and near misses flashed through my mind's eye like a high-speed camera reel when the film strip is released. The Opens, the one-stroke missteps, the second-place finishes, all of it came crashing down on me at once. I was a beaten man. For the second time in my life, I felt like crawling in a hole and never coming back out.

***

The official announced, "Alright, fellas, the five pars are in, congratulations. Beard and Starks–"

"What?" I said to myself, "Not Nate too?"

The official continued, "…to the second tee to play off for first and second alternates."

Nate and I looked at each other and, shaking our heads in disbelief, wandered over to the second tee.

Nate's words "in the wind" and "high and dry" were echoing in my soul. He was trying to scratch out a living on the tour and obligated to a sponsor. I was simply here on a lark. I had a job and was happy. I had left the tour two years earlier, never to look back. I knew what I had to do.

"Nate," I said, "you are the first alternate. I'm going to forfeit."

"Forfeit? What are you talking about?"

"Listen, you've been out here for over ten years. Week after week, you have scratched and clawed your way around this country in search of success. We both know how hard it has been for you out here. I can't imagine what all you have been through. I gave up my dreams two years ago and now have a good life just an hour down the road. You are hundreds of miles from your family and need every opportunity you can get."

"Yeah, but still…."

"Look, alternates get into tournaments all the time. Surely, a couple of the 150 guys who entered the tournament will scratch due to illnesses or other reasons. Al Geiberger's dad just passed away last week in a plane crash in Spain, so you know he will probably not play. So, it's not a big deal. First or second alternate is OK with me, but I want you to have the sure thing."

"Gaines, I don't know what to say."

"You don't have to say anything, pal. I am mailing my application to the USGA on Monday to request my reinstatement as an amateur, no matter what happens this week."

"Thank you, Gaines. You are a hell of a good friend."

"You don't have to thank me, Nate. You probably would have beaten me anyway; I just saved myself the agony."

Laughing, we headed back to the club, sharing stories along the way. We informed the officials of our alternate status and agreed to meet on Tuesday at Forest Oaks Country Club at one o'clock for a practice round. As I drove home that evening, I felt sure that I would get into the tournament.

***

Tuesday turned out to be a day that I will never forget. I got up early and arrived at Forest Oaks around ten. I wanted, for the last time, to soak in all the atmosphere associated with being a professional golfer at a PGA tour event.

Being an alternate gave me the same clubhouse and locker room privileges as the other players. I wanted the opportunity to meet as many of my heroes as I could. All the stars would be there.

I went straight to the putting green so I could rub shoulders with the best players in the world. On the green was Johnny Miller. I had sold him a set of Tommy Armour irons back in 1974 when I was at Possum Trot. Leonard Thompson had been in town one day and saw my Tommy Armour irons and said, "Gaines, Johnny Miller is looking for this exact set. Would you be interested in selling them?"

"Hell yeah, take them and see if he wants them."

Leonard sold them to Johnny for two hundred dollars when they were at the Masters tournament. That very next spring, Miller began 1975 with three victories. He won the Phoenix Open by fourteen strokes, which included a second round of 61. He was twenty-four under par. Johnny then went on to win the Tucson Open by nine strokes with another 61 in the final round.

After a few minutes of putting around him, I got up the nerve to introduce myself.

"Johnny, my name is Gaines Beard. Leonard Thompson sold you a set of Tommy Armour irons that I had back in 1974."

"Hi, Gaines, I remember that. Those were some fine sticks. I wish I had them today."

"What happened to them?"

"I wore them out."

We talked for a few more minutes about the tournaments he had won with them. I couldn't help but think how some of the things we may do in life end up having such an impact on others.

I practiced and hung around the putting green for more than an hour talking with the guys. Some I knew, and some I didn't. I was surprised at how many of them had heard of me. What an ego blast!

After a while, I figured I would check out the locker room. All the players are assigned a locker with their names on it. As a second alternate, I didn't have a locker, so I stood my staff bag up inside the door next to the tour mailbox. The mailbox was a mobile stand with alphabetized pockets that tour players used to receive fan mail and other correspondence. I looked in the "B" slot and saw that I didn't have any fan mail.

In the middle of the locker room stood a banquet table adorned with a plaid tablecloth. On it was all you would expect in a PGA tour locker room: four or five different types of sandwiches and cold cuts. Potato salad, slaw, pickles, and such were on one side of the table and on the other, soft drinks, iced tea, bottled water, and coffee. I decided I was hungry.

I was seated at a small table near the door when Bobby Nichols came in. While he was checking for mail, he looked at my bag and stared at it for a moment.

Bobby Nichols was a premiere player and had twelve wins on tour, including the PGA Championship in 1964. He was a wire-to-wire winner in the PGA and beat second-place finishers Arnold Palmer and Jack Nicklaus by three strokes.

"Whose bag is this?"

"It's mine, Bobby. I'm Gaines Beard, an alternate this week."

"Nice to meet you. Is that the new Zebra putter that just came out?"

"Sure is."

"Mind if I take a look at it?"

"Help yourself," I said, somewhat proud that I had something special in my bag.

He removed the black and white striped sock headcover and took a few practice strokes.

"This thing has great balance. I'm going to have to get me one of these!"

"You want it?"

"Thanks, no. I'm hoping you will need it. Good luck getting in, Gaines."

Original Ram Zebra putter

I finished my lunch and went outside to see an official to find out if anyone had dropped out. On my way to the official's trailer, I ran into Leonard, who was talking to Johnny Miller. As I approached, I caught Leonard's eye. He looked back at Johnny and said, "That is the guy who sold you the Armour irons."

"I know, I've already met Gaines."

"Well," Leonard said, winking at me, "did you give him a cut of the money you won using his clubs?"

"No, but I gave him my autograph on a check."

Chasing A Dream

We had a good laugh, and I had a chance to catch up with Leonard. He told me that he had just heard that a player had scratched and that I was now the first alternate. Hearing that it wasn't Al Geiberger made me feel even better about my chances of getting in.

I was ecstatic for Nate and couldn't wait to see him. I grabbed my bag from the locker room and headed over to the range. It was fun being on the grounds and seeing all the spectators milling around and in the bleachers behind the tee at the driving range. When I got to the range, I found a spot near the right side of the tee. I saw Nate hitting balls four spots over and went up to congratulate him.

"Congratulations, Sarge. I'm now in the hot seat," I said with a grin.

"Thanks again, Gaines. I really appreciate what you did."

"Forget it, pal. I still have the rest of the day for someone to pull out, and there's still Geiberger, you know."

"Yep, it would be nice if you found out today or tomorrow instead of having to come here Thursday and sit on pins and needles waiting for someone not to show up. Man, that's hell. I had to do that last year in Memphis, and I thought I would go out of my mind waiting for a no-show."

"What happened?"

"With only six groups to tee off, a guy had a fender bender and couldn't make his tee time."

"You lucky dog. Did you make the cut?"

"No. Had a couple of bad putting rounds."

"Tell me about it!"

At one o'clock, Nate and I headed over to the first tee to start our practice round. We agreed to play a friendly five-dollar match, which is what we always did. As I was teeing it up, Nate said, "Gaines, I've got a surprise for you."

"What!" I replied as I started my pre-shot routine.

"Lee Elder is going to join us on the back nine."

"You've got to be shittin' me!!!"

In 1974, Lee Elder won the Monsanto Open and received the first-ever invitation given to a black golfer to compete in The Masters. I was going to play with a trailblazer and true champion of the game. Beside myself, I asked, "How the hell did that happen?"

"Lee and I are old friends, and we always try to play practice rounds together whenever we have the chance. He wants to meet you, too."

"Me? Why?"

"You know. Now, hit the ball. We don't have all day."

I was so excited that I almost whiffed my drive. Nate roared with laughter and said, "Lee's going to expect better golf than THAT."

We played a solid front nine. Nate shot a 36, and I beat him two and one to take ten dollars from him with a 34. When we got to the tenth tee, Lee was waiting for us with his caddy. Nate introduced me. "Lee, this is my good friend, Gaines Beard."

I was looking into the kindest eyes I had ever seen and shaking hands with a legend.

"It's a pleasure to meet you, Mr. Elder."

"It's nice to meet you, too. Call me Lee, please. Nate has told me a lot of nice things about you, Gaines. That was an incredible gesture you made yesterday. I don't know many guys who would have done that.

"Thank you, Lee. I hope I don't ruin your game this afternoon with my bad golf."

He laughed and said, "Let's just play golf and have some fun."

Lee, Nate, and I had a great time that afternoon. As we walked together, Lee shared with us a few stories about the discrimination he experienced on the tour.

It was hard to hear about the horrible letters and death threats he had received over the years. In those days, he and his fellow black golfers would have to change their clothes and shoes in the parking lots because blacks weren't allowed in the clubhouses.

Hearing him talk, I knew he was fully aware of the impact his appearance at Augusta in 1975 had on the golfing world. It was a milestone in the fight against racism in our country.

I played solid golf with Lee and Nate. Lee had a self-taught swing, and it was a treat to watch him hit the ball. When we finished, I had shot a 69 and Nate had a 72. Lee shot an effortless 34 for the nine holes.

"Gaines, you strike the ball very well," Lee said. "I'll be on the lookout for you in the future."

"That's mighty kind of you, Lee, but I'm applying for my amateur status on Monday unless someone is a no-show tomorrow; this may have been the last round of my professional career."

"I certainly hope it's not."

"Well, if it is, then I can't think of a better way to hang up my spikes than by playing my last round with you. You too, Nate."

I said my goodbyes and good lucks and headed for the parking lot. On my drive home, I must have smiled the whole way. It was hard to take in the whole day, putting green, locker room, driving range and LEE!" Damn, what a day!

Wednesday was Pro-Am day at Forest Oaks. I spent the day practicing at home in Salisbury, hoping to get word that someone had dropped out of the tournament. I called the official at six that afternoon, and he said that I was still the first alternate. He said to be at the club by 7:30 in the morning, ready to tee it up in case someone was a no-show.

***

I arrived early and had a Danish and a cup of coffee. The "dew sweepers" were getting their things together, putting on their spikes and grabbing a bite before their tee times. I was met by an official who told me he was my contact if someone didn't show.

"Let me know where you are in case we need you."

"You bet I will. Thanks. Have you heard from Al Geiberger?" I asked eagerly.

"Yes, he's in town and scheduled to tee off at 9:50."

You would have thought I had taken a wooden stake to the heart. I'm sure my expression showed my disappointment.

"Keep your chin up. You never know with these things."

Since golfers show up no later than an hour before their tee times, by 9:15, I knew that every player was here at the club for the morning tee times, which were from 7:50 to 10:10.

Nate talked about being on pins and needles, and now I knew what he meant. Time seemed to go by in slow motion, tick tock, tick tock. I just couldn't sit there all day waiting and wishing, I had to move around. I told the official that he could find me either on the putting green or at the driving range.

As I made my way over to the range with a few clubs in my hand, I was approached by a couple of youngsters seeking autographs.

"Are you somebody?" one of them asked.

"I don't know," I replied, looking into their eager eyes. "Who were you looking for?"

"A famous golfer," the other one replied. I smiled and said, "Well, I guess you've found him." I signed their programs and patted them on their heads. They ran away skittishly, and I felt like somebody, if just for a moment.

I hit balls for a while and chatted with a couple of the guys. It was getting close to 9:50, so I took my clubs and went over to the first tee to watch Al Geiberger tee off. I needed to see this with my own eyes.

Al arrived at the tee and greeted his playing partners and the scorers assigned to his threesome. I had read in the morning paper where a reporter had asked Al about playing in the tournament so soon after his father's death. Al said that he thought his father would have wanted him to play. Well, I wasn't his father, and I disagreed. A part of me wished he would suffer a heart attack on his backswing, sending the officials scurrying to find me. It didn't happen and at 1 o'clock, I was informed that the entire field was accounted for.

Well, that was it - the end of the line. I was never going to play professional golf again. In a strange way, I felt relieved. Finally, an end to the pain and suffering that I had endured over the years.

I learned that the word "expectations" often ends up in disappointments. Did I regret not playing the second hole in the playoff? Not for a moment. That Tuesday at Forrest Oaks was a day I will never forget.

I drove home to Salisbury that night a defeated warrior, never to fight again. On Monday, I applied to get my amateur status reinstated.

Chapter 14

The Next Chapter

It was 1978, a year after applying to get my amateur status back. I had closed the doors of my golf discount store and was now working in my family's conveyor manufacturing plant. I was given a job in the shop, punching the clock and learning the business from the ground up.

The previous November, Gracie had given birth to our second son, Marshall Hopkins Beard. We were completely settled down now with a house, two children, and a black lab named Poppy. I was at peace with my past and looked forward to my life as a father, husband, and career builder.

As a new amateur, I played in every golf tournament in Rowan County. I won ten of the eleven events I entered and was a medalist in the two events that required a qualifying round for tournament seeding. The only event I didn't win was the Rowan County Amateur Championship, a match-play event held at Corbin Hills Golf Club. I lost in the finals to Richard Cobb, a young member of Corbin Hills, 2-1. Richard was five under par through seventeen holes, and I was three under.

For the next decade and a half, I was considered one of the best players in the county, with one or more victories each year for thirteen years straight.

I wasn't scared to take my game on the road either. I relished the opportunities to play in state and regional amateur tournaments, many of which were conducted by the Carolinas

Golf Association, a chapter of the United States Golf Association.

As I mentioned earlier, I qualified for the North and South Amateur Championship in Pinehurst, which is my crowning achievement in amateur golf.

I have had many memorable tournaments over the years. I finished seventh in the Mid-South Amateur, also played in Pinehurst. I had two top-ten finishes in the Carolina Mid-Am and one top-ten in the North Carolina Amateur.

I qualified for match play in the Carolinas Four-Ball played in Camden, South Carolina a dozen times and was runner-up once with my partner and former college teammate Allen Craven from Concord, North Carolina.

I finished second low amateur and in the top twenty overall in the 350-player Carolinas Open Championship. There was also the third-place finish in the National Walter Hagen Cancer Championship, played at Walt Disney World after we won the South Carolina Championship in the same event.

Beards qualify for national

MYRTLE BEACH, S. C.— A team led by the Beard brothers — Bryce and Gaines— of Salisbury captured the South Carolina Cancer golf tournament and qualified for the national tourney at Disney World here over the weekend.

Playing with the Beards were Possum Trot pro Harris D'Antignac and Leroy Brunson of Mrytle Beach. They carded a 65 in the first round and came back with a 12-under 60 in the last round to capture the event. Bryce Beard contributed six birdies during the final round. The team was 19 under par for the two days.

The national tourney will be played Dec. 11-12.

Beards lead SC to 3rd in nation

The Salisbury Beard brothers — Bryce and Gaines— lead the South Carolina team to third place in the ninth annual National Walter Hagen Cancer Society golf tournament at the Walt Disney World in Florida over the weekend.

The Beards combined with Harris Dantignac and Leroy Brunson of Myrtle Beach, S. C., to post a two-day total of 131. A bogey on the final hole cost them a chance at the national title. They finished a stroke behind Florida and Georgia which tied for first at 130. Florida then won the crown in a playoff.

Gaines Beard sparked the South Carolinians to a 66 in the first round with four birdies and an eagle.

South Carolina moved into the lead with a birdie on the first hole of the final round and went on to shoot a 65. Bryce Beard had a couple of key birdies. However, a bogey on the last hole in the high wind dropped the SC team into third place.

Chapter 15

The Dogfight

Sometime in the spring of 1995, a golfing buddy of mine told me about a Monday afternoon dogfight that he was going to in Charlotte at the Renaissance Park Golf Club. He said that every week, two to three dozen golfers meet there at one o'clock and play in a "skins" game. He suggested that I should ride along with him and check it out.

A friend of his, Robert Yopp, was running the game by filling out the scorecards, collecting the greens fees and cash for the round and posting the scores afterward.

That was the day I first met Dennis, a 6'-2" handsome young man with blonde hair and blue eyes, with an ingratiating smile, and an athletic build. His eyes were icy blue, and they seemed to always have a welcoming glint to them. He was easy to take to and possessed a charisma that attracted those around him.

This is the story of Dennis McCormac. a young man I met twenty-nine years ago. At the time, Dennis, an affable thirty-one-year-old with a passion for golf, had recently relocated from St. Louis, Missouri, to Charlotte, North Carolina, to start a retail furniture and interior design business with his lovely wife, Jennifer. In St. Louis, Dennis worked for World Sports Promotions, running corporate special events and outings throughout the country. Anheuser-Bush, General Motors, Hasbro, and Coca-Cola were among his major clients.

Later that summer, Dennis took over Robert Yopp's duties running the Monday games. He also started the Amateur Golf Tour and saw the participation grow to more than fifty players playing six tournaments in the fall. In the second year, Dennis needed more golf courses to add to his growing schedule, so he approached Todd Smith of Charlotte Golf Services and laid out his plan for expansion. Smith, who operated three golf courses in the Charlotte market offered the Charlotte Golf Links as the inaugural event of a sixteen-tournament schedule, which Dennis named The Amateur Golf Tour.

Dennis and I became close buddies. With my experience in the professional ranks, Dennis often called on me for help at the scorer's table and with the posting of the scores. He would often ask my opinion about the proper procedures when a rules infraction would occur.

That year, Dennis expanded his tour to include the Raliegh and Greenville, South Carolina regions. The next year, he had more than twenty events running from February through November. He brought on board the Carolina Brewing Company in Mooresville, North Carolina, as a major sponsor. The tour then became the Carolina Blonde Amateur Tour, named for the brewery's flagship brand.

Within months, The Carolina Blonde Amateur Tour had grown to include events in ten cities with the additions of Atlanta, Gastonia, Hilton Head, Fayetteville, Wilmington, Rock Hill, and Myrtle Beach. With the Tour gaining popularity and in so many different cities, Dennis had to engage local "Tour Directors" to run the various events in those cities. The directors would follow Dennis' handbook for running and promoting their events and they were compensated by getting a percentage of the local entry fees.

Chasing A Dream

Being a local director was not a full-time job, and no one did it to make a living. It was, however, enough money to make their time worthwhile and carried with it another financial benefit that does not detract from the purse payout. Most tour directors were granted playing privileges at the courses on which they conducted tournaments. This was a substantial perk, considering club memberships at many of these clubs were thousands of dollars a year.

There were several reasons why his tour was an instant success. He put players in flights with equal abilities according to their USGA-certified handicaps. The rules of golf were strictly adhered to with players found cheating banned from future events. There were no mulligans or do-overs or gimmie putts. It was an opportunity for golfers to play golf as it is intended, by the rules. There was a dress code that didn't allow untucked shirts or blue jeans. Profanity and bad behavior were strictly prohibited.

Dennis would say, "This is a gentlemen's game, and we should act accordingly while guests at these golf clubs." He would often pair me in his group along with two other of his buddies who liked to gamble.

Cliff Cunningham and Mike Emery played with us often early in our relationship. Cliff had a farm near Monroe and really didn't look like your "regular" golfer. He wore a John Deer cap and had a golf towel hanging out of his back pocket. He told me he always used a pull cart when he played at his home course near Monroe.

At the end of the season, Cliff won the tour trophy for most money won that year. When Dennis recognized Cliff with the winner's gift card, he announced,

"For those of you who are not aware, Cliff is the current North Carolina Senior Amateur Champion, having won the championship last year and again this year. You might as well resign yourself to the fact that unless you play your "A" game, he will whip you like a drum and take away your lunch money."

Mike Emory was a very successful retired executive from California. He was a handsome and somewhat stocky fellow with blonde hair. He wore his collar up and sported gold necklaces and a large gold bracelet on his right wrist. On his left wrist was a beautiful gold Rolex watch with a diamond bezel. He was somewhat of a know-it-all, outspoken, and very opinionated.

Both Mike and Cliff were excellent low-handicap golfers and fierce competitors. Dennis and I would have thrilling matches against them and would often go out for an emergency nine after scoring and giving out the awards.

Another great player that I had the privilege of playing with was Andre Springs, a former standout player at Fayetteville State University and golf coach at Livingstone College in Salisbury. I had played in several Rowan County tournaments against Andre during the 1980s and found him to be a fierce and congenial opponent. He had recently won the Greater Charlotte-Metro Amateur Championship and found Dennis' tour to be the best stage to hone his golf skills in a competitive atmosphere. Andre went on to win the tour championship that year.

Dennis rarely met a bet that he didn't accept. Even when the odds seemed stacked against him, he figured he could out-gamble you. He had two powerful weapons in his arsenal: his putter and his 4-iron. Dennis was a very good putter, but better yet, he could read greens like nobody's business. And that 4-iron! Dennis could smash a low bullet-like draw that would go 220-230 yards with deadeye accuracy. In a tight match, Dennis would put aside his driver "ego" and resort to wearing out his opponent by consistently keeping his ball in play with that 4-iron.

Dennis and I liked to gamble so much that we always had a side bet between us even though we were partners in the foursome match. Our usual bet was a twenty-dollar Nassau with automatic two-down presses and a one-down press on holes nine and eighteen. If one of us had won money on the front side, we had the option to double the bet to forty dollars on the back nine. If one of us had a monetary lead going into the last hole, we would often play that hole for double-or-nothing.

Gambling matches like those could make you dig into your squirrel money if you didn't play well. Over the six-year period that I played on Dennis' tour, I doubt there was much money, overall, won or lost between us.

***

After several years, the Carolina Blonde Tour became the Keller-Williams Amateur Tour with sponsorship from the realty giant.

In the fall of 1997, Dennis started a separate Senior Tour in many of the cities he was already in. In the Carolinas, it was known as The Harris Teeter Senior Amateur Tour.

Fast forward to the present day, Dennis' tour is presently sponsored by Golfweek Magazine, a publication of USA TODAY. He has more than eight thousand dues-paying members playing tours in forty-eight cities nationwide. His Senior Tour plays in twenty-five cities. He conducts twelve hundred tournaments a year, eight hundred on the regular tour and four hundred on the senior tour. Dennis, along with his wife Jennifer, run the entire operation out of their home on Hilton Head Island, South Carolina. They have two full-time employees who develop and coordinate their website and various other operational duties. Dennis credits Jennifer with doing the lion's share of the daily operations and accounting.

"I could never have done it without her help," Dennis told me. "She has been the glue that has held this whole thing together through our skyrocketing growth and expansion."

The tour has a podcast, and each tournament has web-based "live scoring" throughout the round. Each October,

Dennis hosts the Tour (s) National Championships in Hilton Head, South Carolina. They play on nine of the finest courses in the area, including Atlantic Dunes, Palmetto Hall, the Golden Bear, the Country Club of Hilton Head, Oyster Reef, Dolphin Head, and Hampton Hall Country Club.

A thousand golfers representing all forty-eight regular tours and five hundred others from the senior tour make the pilgrimage to Hilton Head for this incredible week of golf, competition, and camaraderie. This influx of these players and families into the Hilton Head area makes this event one of the biggest economic boom weeks of the year.

***

Jennifer and Dennis have been married for thirty-three years and have partnered in five different businesses together. They adore one another and have made a magnificent team through the years. The Golfweek Amateur Tour will turn 30 years old in 2024, and the Senior Tour is currently celebrating its 25th anniversary.

"I always knew that Dennis was going to do something special during his career," Jennifer says. "He is so driven, and he's never afraid of taking chances."

I am fortunate to have been a small part of Dennis's story and witnessing it firsthand. I consider Dennis one of my very dear friends. His story is truly a Horatio Alger story of our time. The Golfweek Amateur Golf Tour is the largest amateur tour in the world.

Chasing A Dream

Dennis and Jennifer at the Golfweek Amateur Tour National
Championship
Hilton Head, South Carolina

Chapter 16

The Caddy

Many people think a caddy is a person who carries your bag while you play golf. He carries the bag and keeps the clubs clean. He tends the pin for you and rakes the traps and occasionally might help you read the break of a putt. He holds your umbrella when it rains and keeps your grips dry. He may be a fella who knows the game quite well and is possibly an accomplished player himself, or he may just be a local high school lad making money after school and on weekends.

The basic skill set of a caddy is not difficult to learn or perform. However, that is where the line is drawn between being a caddy and being a CADDY.

My earliest caddying was for my brother, Bryce, while living in Montgomery, Alabama, at the age of twelve. We lived outside the city limits in a rented farmhouse. It was situated on one-hundred-twenty-five acres of pastureland with two ponds and a stream running through it.

About half a mile away was a public golf course, and I would caddy for my brother whenever he played golf there. The course had several ponds on it, and occasionally, Bryce and I would go there in the late afternoon to retrieve balls from them. Since the ponds often had water moccasins, we devised a plan to get balls without wading in the water.

Bryce found a rake in the barn and tied a piece of rope to the handle. We would toss the rake into the pond and slowly pull it back to the edge with the rope. It didn't take long to find enough balls for us to set up our own driving range in the pasture behind the house.

We found three tree limbs that were straight and stuck them in the ground on our range at one hundred, one hundred fifty and two hundred yards. After tying rags to them, we had our own private driving range.

We had plenty of pond balls and would practice hitting balls into the pasture for hours. Afterward, we would have to go and find them in the thick grass. It felt like we were on an Easter egg hunt, and it took a long time.

One day Bryce looked at me and said, "OK, it takes too long to go and find the balls after we hit them, so I'm going to teach you how to shag like I did back in Columbus."

We would take turns shagging for each other and never lost a ball after that.

***

Our stepfather was transferred to Wyoming when I was thirteen. We lived on Francis E. Warren Air Force Base, which adjoined the Cheyenne Country Club. It wasn't long before Bryce and I went over to the club to see if they needed any caddies.

The sign above the pro shop door said the pro's name was Frank Petersen, PGA. Since Bryce was fifteen and had some caddying experience, Mr. Petersen said Bryce could caddy on the weekends. As far as I was concerned, Mr. Petersen said I could come over on the weekends and help as a bagboy with picking up the balls on the driving range.

What a thrill it was to have my first paying job at a golf course. I was there every weekend on time and prided myself on doing a good job. I would pull the member's clubs out of the bag room in the morning then wash the clubs and place them back in storage in the afternoon. After that, I would pick up the range balls before going home.

I found myself caddying for club members while working as a bagboy at the Cheyenne Country Club. I enjoyed caddying because it gave me the opportunity to see how golfers played the game and make some money doing it.

My first introduction to real caddying came as a challenge from Bill Connell, my college golf coach at Wingate College, in 1969. Coach Connell told me that if I wanted to see firsthand how the game was really played, then I should go to the Kemper Open, held at the Quail Hollow Country Club in Charlotte, and sign up to be a stand-by caddy.

In those days, only the elite professionals, roughly a hundred, made enough money to afford their own personal caddy to travel with them from tournament to tournament. That meant that fifty pros out of the one-hundred-fifty-man field would pick up a local caddy at each event. Coach suggested that I go to Quail Hollow early on Monday morning, three days before the tournament began, to ensure my name was on the list in the top fifty spots. I did as he suggested, and on Tuesday morning, I was assigned a young touring pro named Howell Frazier from Panama City, Florida. He was a non-exempt player, which meant he did not have his full tour credentials.

Non-exempt players had to qualify on Monday prior to the event to earn a spot in the field. Once he has qualified, if he plays good enough to make the Friday two-round cut, he'd be among the seventy players advancing to the weekend. Making the cut would guarantee him a check. But more important than that, he would be exempt from having to qualify for the next tournament and automatically in that field. Howell had made the cut the week before and was automatically in the field at the Kemper.

Quail Hollow Country Club is elegant, with multi-million-dollar homes lining its fairways. Howell and I played a practice round on Tuesday and played in the Pro-Am on Wednesday.

Howell played well on Thursday and Friday and made the cut. This was very exciting for both of us because I would get to caddy for two more days, and Howell was guaranteed a payday.

On Saturday, we were in a threesome with Tony Jacklin from England and Dale Douglas from Oklahoma, both stars in that era. Jacklin would go on to win the British Open Championship later that year, and Dale was a member of the 1969 United States Ryder Cup Team.

Both Tony and Dale had their regular caddies, which made me the rookie in the group. Fortunately, I knew enough about caddying to keep me out of harm's way with the rest of the men. I didn't step in anyone's line. I was adept at trap raking, which was noticed by the other two caddies, who occasionally asked me to finish up their raking while marching on with their man.

I didn't mind; in fact, it was a compliment to be asked by a tour caddy to rake his trap for him. The player's caddy is responsible for leaving the trap in as good or better condition than it was before they entered it. For them to trust me to do their job meant I had earned their respect and trust.

Caddying in my first PGA Tour event was certainly an education. I learned a lot that week. I watched and listened more that week than I talked. I observed firsthand the interactions that went on between the caddy and his player. I learned when to be quiet and when to offer comments, observations, encouragement, or help with a club selection. I noticed how caddies knew things like:

- o the rise or drop in elevation of the hole
- o the direction and force of the wind
- o the humidity
- o the wetness or dryness of the course
- o the precise yardages to their targets

The most important talent a caddy must have is the ability to sense his players' confidence and commitment to the shot he is about to hit. It is an absolute fact that if a player has a sense of doubt about the shot about to be played, the result will most likely not be the result he wanted.

Laser focus and confidence are what a caddy tries to instill in his player, his partner! Some of the most important interactions between the player and caddy do not happen when standing at the ball and planning the next shot.

What the caddy says or doesn't say to his man while walking down the fairway can have an incredible bearing on the players' confidence. A good caddy knows his player and how to keep him in a positive frame of mind.

I have had numerous caddie experiences since the Kemper Open in Charlotte. I've caddied on the Ben Hogan tour, now known as the Korn Ferry Tour and the Futures Tour, both stepping-stone tours of the PGA and LPGA tours. I caddied in the 1990 Planters Pat Bradley Invitational on the LPGA tour for Jenny Lindback, a young lady that we housed several years earlier when she played in the Salisbury Classic.

Chasing A Dream

I caddied for a sixteen-year-old young man named Logan Harrell in the 2008 USGA National Junior Amateur Championship at the storied Shoal Creek Club in Birmingham, Alabama. Two years later, at age 18, Logan became the youngest man ever to win the Carolinas Amateur Championship.

Logan at age 16

One of my fondest memories involving caddying did not occur with me being the caddy but rather with me as the player. In 1981, on a whim, I decided I would try to qualify for the prestigious North & South Amateur Championship played since 1901 on the legendary Pinehurst No. 2 course in Pinehurst, North Carolina. It is considered one of the most prestigious amateur championships in the world. Former winners include the likes of Harvey Ward, Jack Nicklaus, Curtis Strange, Gary Hallberg, Corey Pavin, and Davis Love III, just to name a few.

Pinehurst No. 2 was designed by one of the premiere golf course architects of all time, Donald Ross. He called it the best test of golf of over the one hundred courses that he designed. It has large crowned and rolling greens which offer a daunting task, even the most seasoned veteran golfer, when it comes to reading the breaks and slopes of the putts. I was certain that if I were to have a chance of qualifying for the tournament, I would need a local caddy by my side. I had just recently gotten my amateur status back after ten years as a professional and knew that if I called the head professional at the club, he would see to it that his caddy master would accommodate me.

Pinehurst Country Club is noted for its caddy program. There is a course, given by the Caddy Master, that one must pass to earn the green coveralls and cap worn with pride by a Pinehurst caddy. Several old-timers were still carrying bags on a regular basis at Pinehurst. There was Fletcher Gaines, who caddied for Tommy Armour, Gene Sarazin, and my US Open qualifying friend, Curtis Strange. There was Willie McRae, who caddied for many famous people like Yogi Berra, Michael Jordan, and presidents Richard Nixon and Gerald Ford. And there was Jimmy Steed, who was Sam Snead's personal caddy whenever he played in a professional event in North Carolina. Jimmy caddied Sam to victory three times in the North & South Open (professional event) in Pinehurst and for most of his eight Greater Greensboro Open titles in Greensboro, North Carolina.

On the morning of my practice round, I arrived at the caddy master's stand, anxious to meet my caddy and walk those eighteen glorious holes in preparation for my qualifying round.

His name tag read John Grant. He was a very distinguished-looking black gentleman who had risen to the rank of Caddy Master after years of steadfast dedication to the sport and service to those who loved the game.

I extended my hand and said, "Good morning, Mr. Grant. My name is Gaines Beard, and I'm told that you have a caddy on deck for me today and tomorrow."

He smiled and turned his head toward an elderly gentleman clad in green coveralls, leaning back in an old cane bottom chair. They looked at one another, and the old man nodded to Mr. Grant.

"I've got just the man for you, Mr. Beard. This here is Jimmy Steed. He will be giving you his services today." I felt my heart leap when I heard his name. Jimmy Steed was going to be my caddy! I did my best to keep my composure. I introduced myself to Jimmy by saying, "Mr. Steed, your reputation precedes you, sir, and I am honored to have your help." Jimmy smiled and said, "Mr. Beard, it's my pleasure and please call me Jimmy. What do you say we go over to the driving range and warm up a little before we head out?"

I hit a bucket of balls and practiced putting for a few minutes before going to the first tee for our 10:40 tee time. I asked Jimmy if he needed anything, a soda or a snack before we teed off, and he said that he was fine. We teed off, along with two other golfers and their caddies.

Walking the fairways of No. 2 gave me a euphoric feeling, a sense that I was on hallowed ground. I hadn't felt this way in years, not since I was a rookie on the PGA tour back in 1975.

Jimmy and I hit it off right from the get-go. We chatted between shots as we strolled those beautifully manicured fairways lined with pine trees and sandy soil. There isn't any rough to speak of at Pinehurst, not like the majority of the "major" golf courses in the country. Sand and pine needles offered their share of penalty if one's ball strayed from the fairway.

Jimmy and I shared stories about growing up around golf and how it had shaped our lives. Jimmy had a marvelous gift for storytelling. With over fifty years of caddying at Pinehurst for some of the most accomplished golfers in the world, Jimmy was never at a loss for words. I could have listened to him reminisce for hours.

We were on the seventh hole when I asked, "Jimmy, have you ever had a caddying experience that stands out in your mind and makes you laugh to this day when you think about it?"

"I have had some fun times out here over the years," he said, "and one of my favorites happened on the next hole, number eight."

Jimmy explained that it was no secret he had been Sam Snead's caddy at Pinehurst for years. Many of the people he "looped" for would ask him about his experiences with the great "Slammin' Sammy," as he was affectionately known. Sam was considered one of the greatest golfers of all time, with a perfect swing. He had a record 82 wins on the PGA tour.

"Well," Jimmy said, "I was caddying for this man from New Jersey a few years back. He was the kind of man who wasn't very chatty or engaging, and he had an air of superiority about himself and his golf ability. You know the type; some people think they know it all and are hard to please."

I smiled as he continued. "To make matters worse, he called me BOY! He would say, boy, how far did Sam hit the ball on this hole, or boy, what did Sam hit from here? He was obsessed with comparing his abilities to that of Mr. Snead's." Jimmy said that when they got to the eighth tee, the man asked him how far Sam had hit his drive on that hole.

The eighth hole is a par 5 that is reachable in two shots and was considered a birdy hole. It has an elevated green, and beyond it, the ground slopes away at a steep angle.

"The last time Mr. Snead was here, he was getting along in age," Jimmy said to the man. "You and he hit it about the same distance, sir." Jimmy smiled at me and said the man teed up his ball and, with a mighty swing, hit it as hard as he could. The ball soared high and long down the middle of the fairway. He said, "I'll bet the old man didn't hit it that far," as he strutted down the fairway, not waiting for Jimmy to catch up with him.

When they got to the ball, some 280 yards off the tee, the man asked, "Boy, where did Sam hit his drive on this hole?"

Jimmy said, "The last time he played here, he hit his drive near about where you are standing right here." This wasn't what the man wanted to hear after hitting his best drive of the day. "OK," he said, "then what did Sam hit from here to reach the green in two?" Jimmy said he rubbed his chin for a moment and replied, "he hit a solid three-wood from here, sir." Jimmy handed him the three-wood and stood back to watch as the perfectly struck shot sailed over the green.

The man was pissed and slammed his club on the ground and said, "I thought you said he hit a three-wood from here?"

"He did; he knocked it over the green, master," Jimmy said. The man barely spoke a word to him the rest of the day.

"Now THAT was funny," Jimmy said with a big grin.

As luck would have it, I shot an even par 72 the next day and secured one of the twelve spots for entry into the sixty-four-man match play event. It was a huge deal to qualify for the North-South Amateur Championship. Most of the field was there by invitation, based on their world amateur ranking.

In the first match, I was defeated two down with one hole to play by a fine young man named John Kennedy from Wilmington, NC.

Amateur

North And South
at Pinehurst No. 2
Opening Round

Kevin Walsh d. Thomas Gunn, 20th hole; Ronald Stelton d. Gray Tuttle, 2 up; Kevin Klear d. Fred Schneller, 2-1; Mike Stoll d. Mike Greene, 19th hole; Brian Claar d. Mark Gonsalses, 5-4; Eric Lawhon d. William Tuten, 4-3; David O'Kelly d. Hugh Barret, 21st hole; David Kargetta d. Bob Royak, 19th hole.

Dick Siderowf d. Paul Benacchi, 1 up; John Pallot d. Don Koonce, 3-2; Bill Nance d. Greg Nizich, 4-3; Jon Seavey d. Hugh Skelley, 2-1; William Plyler d. Robert Berry, 6-5; Corey Pavin d. Mike Hefner, 4-2; Joe Sadowski d. Lee Troop, 5-4; Charles Bradshaw d. Richard Hall, 1 up.

Todd Roberts d. William Stines, 6-4; Mark Bucek d. Phil Bland, 2-1; John Kennedy d. Gaines Beard, 2-1; Bruce Halstead d. John Kerins, 1-up; Kevin Battersby d. Chuck Cordell, 3-2; Mark Brooks d. James McDermott, 3-2; Evan Schiller d. Jon Riddle, 6-5; Jim Mapel d. Bobby Hathaway, 2 up.

Frank Fuhrer d. Tom Rogan, 6-4; Christian Kling d. Brian Lindley, 20th hole; John Sale d. Alfred Sams Jr., 6-5; John Alvarez d. David Daniels, 6-4; Bill Poirier d. Joel Hirsch, 2-1; Greg Shelton d. Farley Davis, 3-1; Allen Doyle d. Gary Marlowe, 1 up; Curt Byrum d. Tom Walters, 4-2.

Dick Von Tacky d. Jim Robertson, 1 up; Mark Stephens d. Ben Norris, 6-4; David Brogan d. Jeffrey Gottman, 1 up; John Beehler d. Kevin Arnold, 4-2; John Lyons d. Robert Stanger, 2 up; Ray Freeman d. Frank Ford, 2 up; John Erlenbach d. Dave Benham, 4-2; Mark Norman d. Walter Brown, 4-2.

Dale Morey d. Randy Kahn, 1 up; Jonny Doppelt d. Bob Klug, 3-2; Charles Bolling d. Brent Richardson, 6-5; William Hadden d. Kenneth Tarling, 20th hole; Robert Mattiace d. Al Peters, 5-3; R.F. Widener d. Vance Whicker, 2-1; John Ryan d. Mal Galletta, 3-1; Robert Linville d. Jack Van Ess, 4-2.

Nathaniel Crosby d. George Lucas, 4-3; Brad Pritchard d. Lee Burke, 2-1; David Dougherty d. Bill Worbbel, 1 up; Steve Hart d. B.R. Kennington, 5-4; Steve Jones d. Mark Lawrence, 1 up; Tommy Armour d. Robert Zink, 2-1; David Hackstadt d. Eric Hanson, 1 up; Barry McCarty d. Michael Bourne, 3-2.

Donald Allen d. Jeff Robinson, 4-2; Chris Dalrymple d. Thomas Hayes, 2-1; Roy Hunter d. Dick Stimart, 5-4; John Inman d. Greg Clatworthy, 19th hole; John Cregan d. Tom Knox, 1 up; Robert Call d. Gene Howell, 2 up; John Ervasti d. Frank Strafaci, 6-5; Allen Sussel d. Robert Timbrook, 5-4.

Gaines Beard

Caddying Connie Baker to victory in the Futures Tour Salisbury Classic

Connie jumping into my arms after sinking the victory putt on the final hole
Courtesy The Salisbury Post

Chapter 17

A Pro's Golf Tips

Develop a Pre-Shot Routine

    Art Joiner, my boss and Head Professional at Possum Trot, afforded me ample opportunities to play golf and work on my game. He gave me countless tips on how to improve my game. Not all his tutelage centered on the golf swing itself. Much of the knowledge I received from him related to other aspects of the game, such as a working knowledge of the rules and the correct procedures related to those rules. He also taught me about course management.
    Course management refers to the way you should select the most appropriate shot to play given your present situation. Being completely focused on the present shot and weighing the risk/reward of your next swing is crucial to playing your best. However, the most important thing that Art taught me about playing my best was to develop my own pre-shot routine.
    We know that repetitive motions have a direct impact on consistency. The more you do something in the exact same way, the more it becomes second nature using muscle memory. The same can be said of repetitive thought processes. A pre-shot routine is precisely that. Saying the exact same things to yourself in your head as you cross off your checklist prior to making your

stroke. To me, it's like what Kevin Costner did in *For Love of the Game* when he thought in his mind before pitching the baseball; "Clear the Mechanism." It's said that it is impossible to concentrate on more than one thing at a time.

Art taught me a pre-shot routine, so I would only have one thing to concentrate on before every shot. It is the same one, with a little tweaking, that I have used to this day.

My pre-shot routine goes as follows:

TARGET

When I look at my ball in relation to where I want to aim my next shot, I always stand several yards behind the ball and look down the line in which I want it to go. I then pick out a spot (a tuft of grass or a leaf) two to three feet in front of the ball that is on the direct line in which I want the ball to travel. If I hit the ball over the spot I have chosen in front of the ball, I can be sure I started it off in the direction I intended.

STANCE

Stance is where I again utilize the spot that I have selected in front of the ball. It is difficult to know if I'm aligned correctly to a target that is far away AND ninety degrees from where I'm facing. By lining up my clubface and then my stance in relation to the spot in front of me, I have, in essence, moved a target that is far away to several feet in front of me.

My stance itself may vary depending on the type of shot I am trying to hit, i.e., a cut or a draw. My stance may be slightly open for a cut and closed for the draw. Regardless of the shot, the clubface is always aligned to my target spot. When successfully hitting the ball over it I have increased the probability of hitting the ball on my intended line.

HEAD

When I address the ball and look down at it, there are several ways to position my head depending on the type of shot I want to hit.

When I am hitting a straight shot, I look down at the ball and picture t it in the center of a clock face, the point from where the hour and minute hands rotate. I want my head positioned so that my left eye would be toward 9 o'clock and my right toward 3 o'clock. My head is now positioned squarely at the ball and parallel to my intended line.

I then turn my head and chin slightly to the right, causing my left eye to be positioned more at the ball than my right. This accomplishes two things:

- It clears my chin away from contacting my left shoulder on my backswing, thus making it easier to hold my head still during the swing and
- It positions my head slightly behind the ball and in a more positive position to enable me to stay behind the ball during impact.

When I want to hit a right-to-left shot or draw, I must have a slightly inside/out swing path through the ball. By tilting my head slightly to my right shoulder, my left eye is now toward 10 o'clock and my right toward 4 o'clock. (Look at Jordan Speith's setup) This makes it easier to create an inside/out swing path. For a left-to-right shot or fade, I do the opposite by tilting my head toward my left shoulder, thus positioning my left eye toward 8 o'clock and my right toward 2 o'clock.

BALANCE

When addressing the ball, I must bend over slightly from the waist to place the clubhead behind the ball. This, naturally, shifts my weight toward the toes. To return my balance to the middle of my feet, I must bend my knees slightly and feel as though I am resting my bottom on the edge of a bar stool.

It is ideal to have my weight centered through my body to the middle arches of my feet, not toward the toes and not toward the heels. Good, centered balance is essential in making consistent golf swings.

SWING

Now that I have my TARGET, STANCE, HEAD and BALANCE in check, the only thing left is to hit the shot. This is the most important moment in your pre-shot routine.

The last thing you say to yourself at this point should relate to the kind of swing you want to accomplish. It could be something as simple as Tempo. It could be Stay Down if you are prone to looking up or Finish the Swing if you have trouble following through. Or if you have "happy feet" and have trouble staying solid through the shot, think Concrete Feet. Think of your feet in concrete blocks. This thought helps to keep you away from swaying and jumping at the ball.

This is the last thing you think before hitting the ball, so make it important.

As Jim Furyk once said, "Get into the process, not the result."

A pre-shot routine helps keep your mind in the present.

A Few Putting Tips

The putter is the most used club in the bag. If you 2-putt every green, you have putted 36 times. There have been countless great putters in this game: Ben Crenshaw, Jack Nicklaus, Tiger Woods, and the list goes on and on. There are several things that all great putters have in common.

One is, they seldom three-putt. Ben Crenshaw said, "The most important element in putting is pace."

A golfer rarely three putts because he read the break wrong, left or right. He is more likely to three-putt because he hits the ball too short or too long. Having good pace is a key factor in eliminating three-putting.

Another thing is that their putting stroke is their own. There is no such "one size fits all" in the golf swing or in the putting stroke. Steven Pressfield wrote in his novel *The Legend of Bagger Vance*: "You are born with a swing. Your swing is yours and yours alone."

This is somewhat true, but what I think he was saying is that no matter what your stroke looks like, if you can repeat it consistently, over and over again, you will have better control over the outcome.

Surely, you can improve your golf swing and putting strokes by taking lessons from your local PGA Professional, but even then, consistency is your main objective.

They also make almost all of their short putts.

I was on a golfing trip in Scotland several years ago with a group of buddies from Salisbury. My putting was atrocious. I couldn't make a three-footer to save my life. After two days of suffering over the short putts, my roommate, Greg Alcorn, suggested a solution. He put a champagne bottle in the middle of the rug in our hotel room and said, "OK, now get your putter and a ball and let's see how many times in a row you can hit that bottle from four feet."

After fifty in a row, he said, "Stop, that's enough. Now, tell me the difference between here and on the golf course." I thought about it for a while, and it was plain as day.

With a short putt on the putting green, I was trying to lag the ball so that it would "fall" into the cup using gravity. I was concentrating on my line instead of my stroke.

In the hotel room, I was putting at a target and "Hitting the Bottle." Since then, I have been a very good short putter, thanks to my pal changing my mindset.

If you can work to improve your "pace" and "hit the bottle," your putting is sure to improve.

Chipping Tips

First off, unless you are an accomplished player, get rid of any wedge of 58 degrees and higher, Period. These clubs are too difficult to use successfully and will only end up costing you strokes in the long run. The highest lofted wedge in my bag is 56 degrees.

Many amateurs have difficulty with chipping. There are several ways to chip around the greens, and this is one method that I have found to be beneficial for the average golfer.

Stay away from using a high-lofted club unless the pin is tucked close to you. It is better to keep the ball low and running than trying to loft it into the air. Lofted shots often end up being "fat" or "skulled" and are embarrassing, not to mention costly.

Try these methods:

If it is possible to putt the ball from off the green, no matter how far it may be, then putt it. I'm not talking about from 30 yards but from four or five yards or less. There is an old saying that goes something like this: "Your average chip will never be better than your average putt." So, I suggest putting it whenever you can. You won't hit it fat, and you won't skull it.

If the fringe is too high to putt the ball, then you will have to chip it. I have found that the following method can be used with great success.

This method involves the use of the seven iron through the pitching wedge. With all four of these clubs, you will use the exact same swing…your putting stroke. These clubs are longer than your putter, so you will have to choke down on the grip until it feels the same length as your putter. You then address the ball the same way you do when you are putting and stroke the club like a putt. Don't let the fact that the heel of the club is off the ground and the toe of the club near the grass. With a little practice, this will not look so strange. This method is intended to keep the ball low while clearing the fringe between you and the hole, with the ball rolling like a putt after landing on the green.

When you are one pace off the green, use the seven iron. Two paces, the eight iron, three, the nine iron, and four or more, the pitching wedge. It is called a pitching wedge for a reason.

Try this in practice and you may find it a valuable tool in your bag.

Gaines Beard

Bunker Shots

    Bunker shots from fairway bunkers require a clean hit without taking any sand before hitting the ball. It is a sweeping type of swing. However, with greenside bunkers, there are two types of shots that are generally used: The blast shot and the chunk and run.

    I teach the blast shot in a very simple way. Imagine your ball is lying on a one-dollar bill. It sits on the image of George

Washington. Your swing is like a fairway shot that takes a four-to-five-inch divot. In the sand, your divot is the dollar bill. You are not hitting the ball but rather sliding the club under the ball.

You should open your stance, aiming left of the pin and lay the face of the sand wedge open on a line to the pin. The club should enter the sand at the back edge of the bill and exit the sand at the other edge. You will put more spin on the ball the more you use a cut-shot swing path through the impact zone.

It is important to accelerate the clubhead through the dollar bill area. Gary Player, one of the greatest bunker players of all time, said to think about it as if you were "striking a match." This gives you acceleration through the ball, enabling you to finish your swing high as you would any other shot. The blast shot is used when the pin is relatively close to the bunker, however, with practice it can be used on longer bunker shots as well.

'Chunk and run' is a method commonly used for longer bunker shots. The ball is played slightly back in the stance, and the clubface is square. The swing has more of a descending blow when compared to a sweeping swing. Try to enter the sand a few inches behind the ball, again with acceleration. The club will dig into the sand, thus popping the sand with the ball out on a lower trajectory and with very little spin, causing the ball to roll out after landing on the green. If you encounter a fried egg or buried lie in the trap, the chunk and run is generally the shot to play.

One Last Tip

Not too long ago, I watched a movie starring Robert Duvall and Lucas Black titled *Seven Days in Utopia*. The story centers around an old veteran tour pro's efforts to instill confidence into the thoughts and actions of a young aspiring tour player. There were several "gems" of wisdom in the film, however, there is one that I have adopted in my own game and in my teachings.

S.F.T.

<u>SEE IT:</u> This refers to clearly seeing the shot you want to play in your mind's eye and the way you want the ball to fly.

<u>FEEL IT:</u> This refers to feeling the swing that you need to use to hit the shot you have seen in your muscle memory.

<u>TRUST IT:</u> This is trusting that you have seen the correct shot and felt how it feels to hit it.

I have replaced my fifth thought in my pre-shot routine, SWING, with See it, Feel it, Trust it. I also print the three letters on my golf ball.

THE END

Acknowledgments

I would like to thank my wife Nancy who believed in me and constantly encouraged me to write my story. I also owe a debt of gratitude to the members of my writer's workshop; Ellen Salkeld, Tom Spirito, Jane Rankin, Mark Supple, Vickie Larkin, John Stickney, Richard Verdier, and Thomas Williams, and especially Dr. John Walker and Sandre Warren for their tutelage and encouragement. Without them, I would never have written this book.

About the Author

As an Air Force brat, Gaines Beard lived throughout the United States as a child. He is a native North Carolinian with a degree in mechanical engineering from Wingate College. For the past forty-five years, he has worked in the material handling industry, supplying automation to the food, beverage, pharmaceutical and consumer products industries. He has two sons, Spencer and Marshall, and he and his wife Nancy live in Denver, North Carolina. Gaines is also the author of a very interesting children's book called "The Adventures of Captain Snappy and Little Buddy."

Printed in the USA
CPSIA information can be obtained
at www.ICGtesting.com
CBHW070725140524
8328CB00017BB/82